GOD
FOR US

*Rediscovering the
Meaning of Lent and Easter*

BETH BEVIS
SCOTT CAIRNS
KATHLEEN NORRIS
JAMES SCHAAP
LUCI SHAW
RICHARD ROHR
RONALD ROLHEISER
LAUREN F. WINNER

EDITED BY GREG PENNOYER & GREGORY WOLFE

PARACLETE PRESS
BREWSTER, MASSACHUSETTS

2015 First Printing this Edition

God for Us: Rediscovering the Meaning of Lent and Easter - Reader's Edition

Copyright © 2014 by Greg Pennoyer

ISBN 978-1-61261-768-8

The Paraclete Press name and logo (dove on cross) is a trademark of Paraclete Press, Inc.

The Library of Congress has catalogued the original edition of this book as follows:

God for us : rediscovering the meaning of Lent and Easter / contributors, Scott Cairns, Kathleen Norris, James Schaap, Luci Shaw, Richard Rohr, Ronald Rolheiser, Lauren F. Winner ; editors, edited by Greg Pennoyer & Gregory Wolfe.
   pages cm
   Includes bibliographical references.
   ISBN 978-1-61261-379-6 (hard cover-jacket)
   1. Lent—Prayers and devotions. 2. Easter—Prayers and devotions. I. Pennoyer, Greg, editor of compilation.
   BV85.G585 2013
   242'.34—dc23   2013031988

10 9 8 7 6 5 4 3 2 1

Published by Paraclete Press
Brewster, Massachusetts
www.paracletepress.com
Printed in China

Contents

HISTORIES OF THE FEASTS AND FASTS OF LENT
Beth Bevis

Greg
Pennoyer
Preface

L IKE ITS COMPANION VOLUME ON ADVENT
and Christmas, God For Us is the result of a journey that
began in an Anglo-Catholic church on Christmas morning, 1998.
That was my first encounter with the depths of meaning in the
liturgy and the beginning of my acquaintance with the rhythm
of the church calendar. At the same time, it was also a discovery
of visual art's capacity to enrich and complement what we learn
from the written and spoken word.

Much has happened since that Christmas morning. My
exploration of the meaning of the Incarnation helped me to see
the importance of an enfleshed faith. It also made me realize that
in subtle but real ways our religious culture often manifests a
distorted Christianity based on the notion of a God who hates
the body and the world he created. Instead, what I found on
my pilgrimage was a God who through the Incarnation of Jesus
Christ revealed his love for all creation and showed us how to live
"for the life of the world."

This discovery, over a period of time, led me into the ancient
Christian tradition of the Orthodox Church. There I discovered
(as others have done in similar journeys into other Christian
traditions) the short leap from the revelation of "God with us"
in the Advent and Christmas season to "God for us" in the Lent
and Easter season.

Until this discovery, I had not paid much attention to Lent—
and, since it is a preparation for Easter, I did not fully comprehend
the meaning of Easter either. Advent and Christmas were easier to
embrace because of their relative joyfulness and brightness.

The Lenten season was harder to grasp. Lent's reputation as a time for the "denial of the flesh," for self-flagellation and a vaguely spiritualized gloominess, made it much more difficult to engage. But my entrance into Orthodoxy, a set of challenging personal circumstances, and the desire to produce this book impelled me to learn more about what the great Orthodox theologian Alexander Schmemann called the "bright sadness" of the Lenten and Easter season.

If Advent/Christmas is a revelation of God's presence with us, then Lent/Easter is a revelation of God's desire to use all of life for our wholeness and our healing—the revelation that he will pull life from death.

Our ability to understand resurrection, our experience of both a personal Easter as well as the Easter of Christ, is shaped by our stance toward life and what it brings our way. Herein lies the purpose of Lent. Whether it is imposed by circumstances or chosen through spiritual discipline, Lent is about nurturing a posture that holds all things lightly, that ensures that our passions are subject to us and not the other way around.

In Lent we learn that the meaning of life is not dependent upon the fulfillment of our dreams and aspirations. Nor is it lost within our brokenness and self-absorption. That meaning is still there—and it can be found.

Lent cleanses the palate so that we can taste life more fully. It clears the lens so that we can see what we routinely miss within our circumstances.

Lent and Easter reveal the God who is for us in all of life—for our liberation, for our healing, for our wholeness. Lent and Easter remind us that even in death there can be found resurrection.

—GREG PENNOYER

Ronald
Rolheiser, OMI

Introduction

CELEBRATION IS A PARADOXICAL THING. IT LIVES within the tension between anticipation and fulfillment, longing and consummation, the ordinary and the special, work and play.

Seasons of play are sweeter when they follow seasons of work, seasons of consummation are heightened by seasons of longing, and seasons of intimacy grow out of seasons of solitude.

Presence depends upon absence, intimacy upon solitude, play upon work.

In liturgical terms, we fast before we feast.

In our time, we struggle with such paradoxes. Many of our feasts fall flat because there has not been a previous fast. In times past, there was generally a long fast leading up to a feast, and then a joyous celebration afterward.

Today, we have reversed that: there is a long celebration leading up to the feast and a fast afterward.

Take Christmas, for example. The season of Advent, in effect, kicks off the Christmas celebrations. The parties start, the decorations and lights go up, and the Christmas music begins to play. When Christmas finally arrives, we are already saturated and satiated with the delights of the season—we're ready to move on. By Christmas Day, we are ready to go back to ordinary life. The Christmas season used to last until February. Now, realistically, it is over on December 25.

Celebration survives on contradiction. To feast, we must first fast. To come to real consummation, we must first live in longing. To taste specialness, we must first have a sense of what is ordinary.

When fasting, unfulfilled longing, and the ordinary rhythm of life are short-circuited, fatigue of the spirit, boredom, and disappointment invariably replace celebration and we are left with an empty feeling which asks: "Is that all?" But that is because we have short-circuited a process.

I am old enough to have known another time. Like our own, that time too had its faults, but it also had some strengths. One of its strengths was its belief—a lived belief—that feasting depends upon prior fasting.

I have clear memories of the Lenten seasons of my childhood. How strict that season was then! Fast and renunciation: no weddings, no dances, no parties, drinks and desserts only on Sundays, and generally less of everything that constitutes specialness and celebration. Churches were draped in purple. The colors were dark and the mood was penitential, but the feast that followed, Easter, was indeed special.

Lent. We know it is a season within which we are meant to fast, to intensify our longing, and to raise our spiritual temperatures, all through the crucible of non-fulfillment.

But how do we understand Lent?

Sometimes the etymology of a word can be helpful. Lent is derived from an Old English word meaning springtime. In Latin, lente means slowly. Therefore, Lent points to the coming of spring, and it invites us to slow down our lives so as to be able to take stock of ourselves. While that captures some of the traditional meaning of Lent, the popular mindset generally has a different focus, looking at Lent mostly as a season within which we are asked to refrain from certain normal, healthy pleasures so as to better ready ourselves for the feast of Easter.

To further our understanding, perhaps the foremost image for this is the biblical idea of the desert. Jesus, we are told, in order to prepare for his public ministry, went voluntarily into the desert for forty days and forty nights, during which time he took no food, and, as the Gospel of Mark tells us, was put to the test by Satan, was with the wild animals, and was looked after by the angels.

Clearly this text is not to be taken literally to mean that for forty days Jesus took no food, but that he deprived himself of all the normal supports that protected him from feeling, full-force, his vulnerability, dependence, and need to surrender in deeper trust to God the Father. And in doing this, we are told, he found himself hungry and consequently vulnerable to temptations from the devil; but also, by that same token, he was more open to the Father.

Lent has for the most part been understood as a time of us to imitate this, to metaphorically spend forty days in the desert like Jesus, unprotected by normal nourishment so as to have to face "Satan" and the "wild animals" and see whether the "angels" will indeed come and look after us when we reach that point where we can no longer look after ourselves.

For us, Satan and wild animals refer particularly to the chaos inside of us that normally we either deny or simply refuse to face: our paranoia, our anger, our jealousies, our distance from others, our fantasies, our grandiosity, our addictions, our unresolved hurts, our sexual complexity, our incapacity to really pray, our faith doubts, and our dark secrets.

The normal "food" that we eat (distractions, busyness, entertainment, ordinary life) works to shield us from the deeper chaos that lurks beneath the surface of our lives.

Lent invites us to stop eating, so to speak, whatever protects us from having to face the desert that is inside of us. It invites us to feel our smallness, to feel our vulnerability, to feel our fears, and to open ourselves to the chaos of the desert so that we can finally give the angels a chance to feed us.

That is a rich biblical image for Lent, but human experience, anthropology, and our ancient myths offer their own testimony.

For example, in every culture, there are ancient stories and myths that teach that all of us, at times, have to sit in the ashes. We all know, for example, the story of Cinderella. The name itself literally means, the little girl (puella) who sits in the ashes (cinders). The moral of the story is clear: before you get to be beautiful, before you get to marry the prince or princess, before you get to go to the great feast, you must first spend some lonely time in the ashes, humbled, smudged, tending to duty, unglamorous, waiting.

Lent is that season, a time to sit in the ashes. It is not incidental that many of us begin Lent by marking our foreheads with ashes.

There is also the rich image, found in some ancient mythologies, of letting our tears reconnect us with the flow of the water of life and of letting our tears reconnect us to the origins of life. Tears, as we know, are saltwater. That is not without deep significance. The oceans too are saltwater and, as we know too, all life takes its origins there.

And so we have the mystical and poetic idea that tears reconnect us to the origins of life, that tears regenerate us, that tears cleanse us in a life-giving way, and that tears deepen the soul by letting it literally taste the origins of life.

Given the truth of that (and we have all experienced that truth), tears too are a desert to be entered into as a Lenten practice, a vehicle to reach new depths of soul.

Lent. It is a season to slowly prepare our souls. It is a time to open ourselves to the presence of God in our lives and let the angels feed us. It is a time to sit among the ashes, confident that love will abound in due time. It is a time to be washed by our tears into the water of new life, to come to real transformation and newness ready to celebrate the feast that is given us at Easter.

Beth Bevis
The Feasts and Fasts of Lent

T HE CHURCH ARRIVES AT EASTER, THE OLDEST and most sacred feast of the Christian year, by way of a fast. Like Advent, the season of Lent has given Christians throughout history a period of time to prepare for the coming holiday through practices of reflection, repentance, prayer, and self-restraint. One of the goals of this season is to reveal habits or mindsets that may be preventing us from experiencing true freedom and wholeness. The restrictions imposed by the Lenten fast seek not to deny the goodness of the many blessings we enjoy in this life, but rather to remind us that they are, in fact, gifts. Above all, a fast is intended to nurture a sense of gratitude to the giver and to encourage us to share these gifts with those in need.

The function of the church calendar is to enact a sense of wholeness and proportion in time, setting aside certain days and seasons for fasting and preparation, others for feasting and celebration. It can be easy to fall into the trap of emphasizing one aspect of the Christian life over all others—to dwell too long on our failures or to embrace only the good news of deliverance from sin, to deny the body or to become complacent about it. Without an intentional guide, such as the one provided by the church calendar, we can lose sight of the full extent of our humanity. The liturgical calendar, with its cycle of festivals and fasts alternating with seasons of "Ordinary Time," helps us to remember not only the breadth of Christian teaching but also what it means to be human, both fallen and redeemed by God.

By the fourth century, when the church officially instituted the forty-day season of Lent, customs of fasting and penance had already begun taking shape among baptismal candidates as a way of preparing for entry into the church at Easter, the usual day for baptism in the early church. With the creation of Lent, the church brought together many of these preexisting customs and directed them to a common need—not only among those entering the life of the church for the first time, but also among practicing Christians for whom the mystery of Easter might threaten to become a mere commonplace.

Lent became a way for Christians to mindfully prepare for the coming feast, to open themselves to their own spiritual hunger in order to make room for the life and fulfillment offered at Easter.

Because Lent is a fast, one might be surprised to find there are many rich traditions associated with the season—traditions belonging not only to the feast days and Sundays that punctuate Lent, but to the fast itself. To be sure, sensory experience is pared down during Lent, but this doesn't mean that it is a time of spiritual dryness. There can be as much meaning in a strategically instituted silence as there is in a resounding "alleluia," as much to glean from a spare Lenten meal as from an Easter feast.

The aim of the histories that follow is to demonstrate the richness of the customs of Lent and to reclaim this season as a time of spiritual renewal that enhances our understanding of Easter, making us readier than ever to embrace the abundant life that Christ made possible for us through his death and resurrection.

A Note about the Dating of Easter

For almost as long as the church has observed Easter the question of how to calculate its precise date has been a point of debate. This has been partly the result of juggling two calendars—lunar and solar—along with the Jewish festival cycle upon which Easter's date was based, since the first Easter took place during the season of Passover. The Council of Nicea in 325 attempted to solidify a universal date, and the replacement of the Julian with the new Gregorian calendar in the sixteenth and seventeenth centuries went some way toward getting the Christian world on the same calendar. But even now, the churches of the East and West calculate Easter's date slightly differently: the Western church sets Easter on the Sunday after the first full moon of the spring equinox (March 21), while the Eastern church still uses the Julian calendar in its calculations. The result is that Christians in the East and West usually celebrate Easter on different Sundays. Many of the customs associated with the feast in the East and West, however, stem from the same early church traditions, and we feature many of them in the coming pages.

SHROVE TUESDAY AND THE FIRST WEEK OF
LENT

Beth Bevis

History of the Feast

Shrove Tuesday
(also known as Pancake Day,
Mardi Gras, or Fat Tuesday)

W HEN IT WAS FIRST OBSERVED IN ENGLAND
in medieval times, Shrove Tuesday was seen primarily
as a day for the confession of sins in anticipation of Lent, which
began on the following day. "Shrove" comes from the Old English
verb "shrive," to impart penance and absolution. Over time, as
the entire season of Lent came to be devoted to the practices of
confession and repentance, the imperative to confess before Lent
was downplayed, and Shrove Tuesday, along with the preceding
week, came to be more focused on feasting and merrymaking,
practices restricted during Lent.

In this way, Shrovetide was similar to its European counterpart,
Carnival, which also originated in the Middle Ages as a pre-
Lenten period of feasting and frivolity, culminating on the Tuesday
before Lent. Carnival traditions have varied over time and place,
but almost always involve the eating of cakes, pancakes, or other
pastries as a way of using up eggs, butter, milk, and sugar—foods
that were at one time prohibited during Lent. Shrove Tuesday's
French name, Mardi Gras or "Fat Tuesday," reflects this history,
as does its traditional name in England, Pancake Day. Christians
in the Eastern Church likewise enjoy meatfare and cheesefare
week, two weeks devoted to soon-to-be-forbidden foods. The
word "carnival" likely originated from the Latin "carne levare,"
signifying the "removal of meat" from the Lenten diet.

As a "farewell to flesh" in an even broader sense, Carnival has
historically involved indulgence in pleasure and a loosening of

social restrictions. In addition to consuming rich food and drink, it was common throughout Renaissance Europe for people to throw mud, flour, eggs, lemons, or other projectiles at each other. At its height in the fourteenth and fifteenth centuries, Carnival focused on satirical performance, including the wearing of masks; in some places, the lower classes would dress up as members of the ruling class in a temporary, humorous role-reversal (reminding everyone of their equality in the eyes of God).

By the nineteenth century, the more disorderly Carnival customs had evolved into new traditions, such as flower battles, masked balls, and parades. Variations on these celebrations can be found today in Europe and in the Americas, where Carnival was introduced by European colonists and where it combined with indigenous cultures to form new traditions, including the famous Mardi Gras parades in New Orleans.

Because Carnival celebrations easily devolved into overindulgence and unrestrained revelry, the Protestant church after the Reformation discontinued the celebration of Carnival, though it kept the observance of Lent. The Catholic Church, on the other hand, continued to allow Carnival but made a concerted effort to curb its excesses. While the dangers of excess are obvious, the Catholic Church recognized the benefit of setting aside time for festivity and feasting before a season like Lent. Just as feasting can be taken to an extreme, with people using Carnival as a license for intemperance or sin, so too can fasting and contrition become excessive if they are not undertaken in light of what Shrovetide and Carnival represent. These days are the Church's way of giving merriment its due place alongside the more ascetic seasons of the church calendar. Culminating on Shrove Tuesday, the festive days leading up to Lent are a vital reminder that there is room in the church calendar—and in the Christian life—for both feasting and fasting.

Richard Rohr, OFM

SCRIPTURE

Isaiah 2:1–5;
Psalm 121;
Romans 13:11–14;
Matthew 24:37–44

THE DAY BEFORE THE BEGINNING OF LENT created a number of local customs in different areas, none of them official but differing from culture to culture. Most of them had to do with hearty eating and drinking before the formal fast of Lent began on Ash Wednesday. Many of us are familiar with the names Mardi Gras (Fat Tuesday) in French speaking countries, Carnival ("letting go of the meat") in Spanish and Portuguese speaking countries, and Pancake Day in many Northern European countries.

Most of these continue to this day and have even grown larger, which seems to reveal some deep need for breaking the rules, going to excess, or coloring outside the lines. Perhaps the tendency toward excess is itself an acknowledgment that the lines are there for a reason.

I once attended an awesome Fastnacht celebration in Calvinist Basel, Switzerland, where the Catholic revelry from before the Reformation was balanced out by measured and beautiful marching, quiet drumming, flute playing, and gorgeous costumes moving in all directions for three nonstop days. Here, too, was excess, but now an excess of order and discipline and creativity—and for a healing purpose.

Like a good Swiss watch, it all began simultaneously and ended simul-taneously in every part of town. The too muchness, as it were, was contained inside very strict boundaries and limits. Similarly, my New Orleans classmates told me that the festivities of Mardi Gras were required to end at exactly twelve midnight—and then the old French Catholics would fittingly get their ashes of repentance the next morning. Both fit into the cycle of life.

However, the church did not attach spiritual significance to this day, and so there were never any formal scriptures or liturgy for what was informally called Shrove Tuesday. Our word Lent came from the Middle English word lente for the season of spring, which corresponded to the forty days preceding the rebirth of Easter, at least in the northern hemisphere (see history of this feast day).

Rather than condemn or idealize either swing of the pendulum—too much fasting or too much feasting—perhaps this is a day to help us recognize that both have something good to offer us. *Preacher*

Even the rather dour Qoheleth, who eagerly condemned all "vanities" in his book of Ecclesiastes, says, as if to balance himself out, "Joy then is the object of my praise, since under the sun there is no happiness for humanity except in eating, drinking, and pleasure. This is our standby during our toil through all the days of life that God has given us under the sun."

If I were to suggest a scripture for today it might also be Qoheleth's most quoted line from earlier in this same biblical text: "There is a season for everything, a time for every occupation under heaven.... A time for laughter, a time for mourning, a time for dancing."

Here is where he first tries to balance out his own pessimism and moralism by recognizing that all things indeed have their time and place. (Of course the list is much longer than we have here; if you wish to see all the truthful contraries that he balances and compares, see Ecclesiastes 3:1–8).

A New Testament scripture might be this: "The time has come, the kingdom of God is now at hand. Change and believe the good news."

Jesus's very first words in the Gospels are a call to change. Isn't it strange that so much of the religion formed in his revolutionary name has been a love of the past and a protection of the status quo?

Lent is intended to lead us into an always hidden future and an always greater opportunity, and it is in truth—a future created by God—but still unknown to us. We now enter Lent with a new and open horizon, ready to both expect and work for God's ever new springtime.

> God of all seasons, God of both feasting and fasting, you guide us through the letting goes and the new beginnings of our lives. We confess to you our weakness in doing this fully, and we ask that we can let go of all impediments to our journey toward "life and life more abundantly" so that we can begin anew in grace. May we never lose hope in the eternal spring that you have promised to all of creation in a "new heaven and a new earth." Amen.

S INCE THE SEVENTH CENTURY, THE WESTERN church has observed the start of Lent on Ash Wednesday—the fortieth day before Easter, not counting Sundays. In addition to providing ample time for self-examination and spiritual reorientation, the duration of forty days symbolically aligns Lent with biblical examples of preparation, fasting, and journeying toward liberation—recalling, for instance, Jesus's forty days of fasting in the wilderness before beginning his ministry, as well as the Israelites' forty years of desert-wandering before their deliverance into the Promised Land. Among most traditions, this first day of Lent is set aside as a special day of fasting; the Roman Catholic Church, for example, allows for the consumption of one meal or two small meals on Ash Wednesday, setting this day aside, with Good Friday, for more rigorous fasting.

Ash Wednesday services are solemn occasions, offering time for prayer, silent reflection, and in some cases confession. The primary feature of the Ash Wednesday service is the imposition of ashes, in which congregants receive a smudge of ashes in the shape of a cross on their foreheads—a sign of humility and repentance. While forming the cross, the minister typically recites God's words to Adam and Eve as they were expelled from the garden: "Remember that you are dust, and to dust you shall return." This ritual reminds us of the inevitability of death, making the hope of Easter and the Resurrection all the more vital. The ashes are also a token of our own status as sinners—an acknowledgment that we, too, have been figuratively exiled and are in need of forgiveness.

The imposition of ashes, now a familiar Ash Wednesday tradition in Catholic, Anglican, and many Protestant churches, has its roots in an early-church penitential practice. For people who had been excluded from the church for serious sin, the imposition of ashes at the start of Lent served as a public sign of their repentance. These sinners then undertook acts of penance throughout Lent and were formally restored to the church community at Easter. By the end of the eleventh century this practice had became less directed to particular kinds of sinners, and the imposition of ashes was prescribed for all Christians in the Western church at the beginning of Lent—a season that was becoming increasingly focused on repentance.

Because Eastern Orthodox Christians follow a slightly different calendar, they do not observe Ash Wednesday, but begin Lent instead on the evening of the seventh Sunday before Easter, known as Forgiveness Sunday. The next day, the first day of Lent, is known as Clean Monday, or Ash Monday by analogy to the Western tradition (although most Eastern churches do not practice the imposition of ashes). In general, the atmosphere of Clean Monday is more celebratory than that of Ash Wednesday. Families in Greece gather in the open air for picnics and enjoy permissible Lenten foods, children fly kites, and there is even dancing on this day. During Clean Week, which begins with Clean Monday, the streets are cleaned of the remnants of the celebrations of Carnival. This literal act of purification can be a reminder that Lent, with its prescribed practices of confession, repentance, and fasting, is meant to assist in the process of cleaning our hearts and preparing our spirits for the celebration of Easter.

Richard
Rohr, OFM

Ash Wednesday

SCRIPTURE

Psalm 103 or 103:8–14;
Joel 2:1–2, 12–17;
Isaiah 58:1–12;
2 Corinthians 5:20b–6:10;
Matthew 6:1–6, 16–21

I N MY STUDIES OF THE NEARLY UNIVERSAL practice of male initiation in native societies, one pattern was so consistent that you knew it had to be proceeding from the deep unconscious and the Holy Spirit. Again and again I read that among Africans, Aboriginal Australians, the old Celts, and Native Americans the young man whose arrogant posturing was deemed dangerous for the community was in various ways forced into immediate contact with his own death. This took the form of making him connect to the earth (humus) to remind him of his humanity and teach him humility. He was often signed with the ashes of death to give him sympathy for the humanity he shared with others and a desire for the full glory of life.

In fact, the very lines from Genesis 3:19 that some churches still use during the imposition of ashes on this feast/fast day, written perhaps five hundred years before Christ, are very likely from these even more ancient rites of initiation: "Dust you are, and unto dust you shall return."

We are beautifully prepared for this psychic shock today by three rather graphic and effective scripture readings used in the Common Lectionary. The prophet Joel poetically and dramatically tells us "to rend our hearts and not our garments," revealing an early Jewish movement toward interiority and purification of one's real motivation. No one will ever be able to ask such an enlightened people, "Where is their God?" Such a God will be obvious and victorious—through and in peoples' changed hearts and lives.

Then dear and inspired Paul says a few amazing things in two very small paragraphs. First, he claims the name "ambassador" for those who are transformed by Christ. He says, "God, as it were, is appealing to the world *through us*!" This man comprehends the full extent of the incarnation mystery before almost anyone else. In the time before any of the Gospels are written, Paul understands how the transference of life and love must take place from God, to Jesus, to us.

And then he adds to that what much of the church still avoids and even denies—that it all happens *now*. "Now is the acceptable time! Now is the day of salvation!" This gift of enlightenment, transformation, and "salvation" is not an evacuation plan for the next world, but a gift of "reconciliation" for this world here and now.

And how did Jesus accomplish this reconciliation? By changing sides and identifying not with righteousness where few could honestly climb up to God but with *sin itself* where all of us have lived.

If I had written this line on my own, I would be accused of heresy or blasphemy, or both. But Paul not only says that God "made" Jesus into "sin" but then further says that he did this so that "we might become the very holiness of God."

Our only holiness, it seems, is God's capacity to include us in his capacity for inclusivity. We are not that holy, but God is, and this is the merciful message that can reconcile the whole world. It is precisely God's forgiving nature which allows him to *incorporate the negative* and thus transform us—in and through and with him.

When we can join God there and do the same, we are divine ambassadors indeed.

But getting to that place can be difficult. One of the main obstacles on this journey is *dualism*, which is built into the very way we think. Our minds tend to work in binaries, by comparison or in contradistinction to another thought, word, or idea. Dualism teaches how to say what something *isn't* before we learn to experience it *in itself*, which is what I mean in part by non-dualistic thinking.

Authentic God experience, which is literally "incomparable," gives saints and mystics a crash course in transcending dualism.

After such momentous proclamations, the Gospel itself shifts gears into something resembling comic relief or satire, where we are chided into remembering that our actions must be focused on inward change rather than public ostentation. On the one day that our faces are liturgically and publicly smeared with ashes, we are then told to wash our faces so no one will know we are fasting. On the one day when so many people come to public services without any church obligation to do so, we are told not to pray in public where others can see us. And on one of the few weekdays when a collection is taken up, we are told that in giving alms we are not to let the left hand know what the right hand is doing.

I always wonder what preachers do with this Gospel in this context and on this day? I surely hope it does not reveal our immense capacity for missing the point.

Inclusive God, merciful God, God of the inner heart, lead us beyond mere external religion and "blowing of trumpets" that merely exalts ourselves. Teach us instead to love you, you who alone are good, all good, and in every good. You make us good in spite of our denials and defenses. And that is why we love you. Amen.

Thursday after Ash Wednesday

SCRIPTURE
Psalm 1;
Deuteronomy 30:15–20;
Luke 9:18–25

TODAY'S FIRST READING FROM DEUTERONOMY sets the bar for all later prophetic teaching. The prophet always makes the choice very clear and usually very demanding, as Moses surely does here. But note that it is all for the sake of "long life" and "blessing," not just for moral gymnastics or later rewards.

It seems that we first have to make a *fundamental option* for life instead of death to get us even started on the spiritual journey. "I do want to be a good and productive person" is a necessary first decision that your own heart must hear and on some level choose. It sets you on the right course, but that is all. It is still all about you.

Such prophetic thinking, however, makes your choice and direction clear for you, and that is good and necessary. I call this *dualistic thinking*. We will see that Jesus does the same when he says, "You cannot serve both God and mammon," or when he calls us to choose the side of either the sheep or the goats, or especially in today's Gospel where he clearly talks about either "saving your life" or "losing it." If you stop right there, however, you will usually end up with rather rigid religion or arrogant moral positions, invariably presuming you are on the right side of the choice—of course!

And many people do stop right there.

So the wonderful thing about the entire biblical revelation is that it includes in its texts both dualistic and non-dualistic teachings. The first ones get you into the right boxing ring—life instead of death. But only then is the real spiritual combat beginning. Now you must spend the rest of your adult life discerning: And what then is life? Divine life? Now? Here? For me? In this context?

Only non-dualistic thinking—mystical or prayerful conscious-ness—can help us here. Up to this point in history, the focus in organized religion has been largely on religious services, or the nature of their authority, along with moral do's and don'ts.

This is a good and usually necessary start, but henceforth it becomes too small an arena in which to really encounter the divine, or for that matter, ourselves.

I call this deeper, prayerful consciousness "second half of life spirituality." The truth is that many people never go there, spending their whole life answering first half of life questions, which are the lowest in the hierarchy of needs—security, status, and the maintenance of self-image.

This is why Jesus's rather brutal words are put right on this second day of Lent. He is saying that our attachment to our self-image, especially any need to think of ourselves as superior, must *die* (some form of this teaching is found from almost all great spiritual masters).

It is a hard-won battle.

Jesus's way of putting it is familiar to most of us although also rather hard to make into a life agenda, because it is so counterintuitive: "Whoever wishes to save his life must lose it, and whoever loses his life . . . will save it." This is his familiar way of talking in paradoxes and riddles, which can only be heard in any meaningful way if you switch to non-dualistic consciousness, or what some call the contemplative mind.

These two readings get us off to an excellent Lenten start, with both dual and non-dual thinking being affirmed in today's two readings. You need both. The first is not bad at all, it is just inadequate to the greater issues of life, love, death, suffering, God, and infinity. Once you move to these inherently spiritual issues, only the contemplative mind is of much use. Life is no longer seen in competing polarities, but in a larger wholeness that many call *wisdom*. Both saving life and losing life are still talking about life—not death. As Ken Wilber says, "The fact that life and death are 'not two' is extremely difficult to grasp, not because it is so complex, but because it is so simple."

For the rest of Lent we will be trying to live inside of this creative tension and paradox.

> God of life and death, teach us to hold out for a deeper life, for the prayerful consciousness that enables us to transcend our petty needs for security and self-image, so that we may be free to rest in communion with you. We do want life, but we want the Big Life, which includes you and everything else too. Amen.

S C R I P T U R E
Psalm 51:1–10;
Isaiah 58:1–9a;
Matthew 9:10–17

THE THEME TODAY, BEING THE FIRST FRIDAY OF Lent which is normally considered a fast day, is clearly fasting itself. Fasting is not something commonly understood, or spiritually practiced in the Western world, so maybe these two readings can give us some good and positive leads. Maybe it is something we can rediscover and recognize that it is much deeper than mere dieting, some form of self-punishment, or any earning of merit.

Isaiah 58:1–9 starts us off by giving us some good leads for a biblical and spiritual understanding of fasting. "This is the fasting that I wish: releasing those bound unjustly, untying the thongs of the yoke, setting free the oppressed, breaking every yoke, sharing your bread with the hungry, sheltering the oppressed and the homeless, clothing the naked when you see them, and not turning your back on your own."

Many of these later became what Christians called the "corporal works of mercy." But what we first of all notice is that they have nothing to do with self-improvement, self-punishment, or the self at all—but always others.

Then, even more positively, Jesus uses the occasion when the disciples of John question him about *not* fasting, and instead of being either didactic or defensive, he actually changes the subject and utterly reframes the question—as he often does. In fact, he introduces two lovely new words into the vocabulary, "wedding guests" and "bridegroom." How amazing is that? It shows us that he is far from criticizing, justifying, defending, or imposing any discipline of fasting.

In fact, he is revealing here his most common metaphor for eternal life or the hereafter. And that metaphor is again and again *a wedding banquet*—at which he himself is God's gracious host or "groom" and we are the marriage partner. It is daring language, but a worldview that he seems to be entirely comfortable with.

Note for example in Luke 14:7–24 that he again uses three examples in a row of parties, guests, and wedding celebrations as his images of eternity. Each of them describe God as a magnanimous host, warning us against any stinginess or exclusion, and in fact telling us to invite not those who can pay us back but "the poor, the crippled, the blind, and the lame."

This is how Jesus understands fasting, fasting from our prejudices, our superiority, and our ethnic divisions. A wedding banquet allows for no fasting whatsoever in the normal sense— quite the opposite. He is clearly recommending feasting instead of fasting. In fact, one wonders how you could miss the point— unless you are stuck in an ascetical mindset.

Jesus is inviting humanity to a common celebration at which all are invited, and the only fasting needed is from our fears and divisions. He extends this point when he finally offers fasting as almost a concession or a prediction of what is likely to come. He says in effect, in my paraphrase of Luke 9:14,15: "You should not do it as long as I am around at the wedding feast, but when

I am taken away, you probably will fast in mourning and grief, but I am neither for it or against it."

There is a place for fasting, and humans do need liturgies of lamentation in times of grief, but God does not need our fasting. Maybe we do, especially in this addictive society, but of itself it does not bring us into deeper union with God.

This is not to say fasting does not have spiritual value or significance, but it is apparently not in Jesus's practice, since he is precisely criticized for *not* fasting by the disciples of John the Baptist. To be quite honest, we find almost no encouragement of asceticism as such in Jesus's teaching. His emphasis is always on the positive, channeling desire, and knowing what you love— not what you are against or avoiding, which only encourages a religion of purity codes instead of his wonderful wedding banquet, the one we can experience both now and later.

Gracious Host, Loving Bridegroom, eternal wedding banquet God, show us when we need to fast and when we need to begin the eternal feast. Keep the party open, and help us not to close it down. Show us that the only fast we need is from ourselves, our smallness, and from our shriveled hearts. Amen.

SCRIPTURE

Psalm 86:1–11;
Isaiah 58:9b–14;
Luke 5:27–32

TODAY THE ARGUMENTS OF YESTERDAY ARE taken one step further as the text from Isaiah continues. His positive understanding of fasting from oppression, false accusation, and malicious speech will lead to immense personal and corporate fruitfulness, according to the prophet. "You will be like a watered garden, like a spring whose water never fails, the ancient ruins shall be rebuilt for your sake." In fact, it will lead you to be "repairers of breaches" and "restorer of ruined homesteads," which are marvelous images for people who can build bridges between opposing ideas and groups, and rebuild society itself.

Then in the well-chosen complementary Gospel, we have Jesus himself crossing cultural and religious boundaries, and inviting a Roman sympathizer to join his inner group, and then (against Jewish practice) even joining him in "a great reception" in his house. Remember, this is a totally unacceptable tax collector, Levi, in the class of objective "sinners," who takes money from his own people to give to their Roman oppressors. Jesus is quickly, predictably, and even appropriately accused of "eating and drinking with sinners and non-observers of the law."

He has broken the simplistic purity codes of early-stage religion, and is being publicly questioned with a criticism that would be very plausible to the crowd. His answer, of course, is brilliant and reveals his entire life agenda of healing: "I have not come for the self-righteous, but for the sick," he says.

Thus Jesus shows himself to be a "repairer of breaches" and a "restorer of ruined homesteads" himself. He is exactly fulfilling the fruitful promise of Isaiah. He is himself fasting from any "false accusations and malicious speech" and "rebuilding the ancient ruins" of his religion. It is hard to interpret the confluence of these two readings in any other way.

Jesus makes clear here and elsewhere that he did not come to create any kind of country club religion. He is not into in-groups and out-groups, but operates throughout his ministry in a consistently inclusive way, often scandalously so to his own contemporaries, as we see in today's Gospel. From later Christian practice, one must conclude that Jesus totally changed his policy and practices after his Resurrection! Do we have two different Jesuses? One who includes sinners and another who is known for exclusion of all types of "outsiders"?

There is a lot of evidence that we do, and maybe that is why both Judaism and Christianity have *not* been known historically or culturally as "repairers of breaches" or "restorers of ruined homesteads" for others. Christians largely ignored the actual historical Jesus and his living message in favor of Jesus as an available religious icon to be worshiped. It created a religious in-group.

But remember, Jesus never said "worship me," and he did say "follow me" in our Gospel today, and many times elsewhere. And notice that he says this to an outsider—Levi, a Roman sympathizer—and not to someone who was already on his side. Like President Lincoln he seemed to want to create a "team of rivals" with his very similar invites of a Leftist zealot Simon, a critic called Judas, and James and John who were called "sons of thunder."

I think it has always been much easier to worship Jesus than to follow him. That demands care for the supposedly unworthy, the sinners, the outsiders, and "the non-observers of the law." Such a lifestyle makes you few friends. When religion remains a mere belonging system instead of a transformation system it becomes a closed country club for the healthy instead of an always-open hospital for the ailing and weak—which is just about all of us.

Jesus says it succinctly: "The healthy do not need a doctor, sick people do." And that is precisely who and what he came for.

> God of all people, God of all creation, God revealed in Jesus, we come to you asking that you expand and open our narrow hearts. Show us a way of salvation for all people, teach us how to build a world that cares for the sick and the outsider and not just for the seemingly healthy. Help us never to conclude that because they are like us, their journey is finished. Help us not to see your message as in competition with other religions, but one that can build bridges to all religions and cultures. Amen.

Beth Bevis

History of the Feast

First Sunday of Lent

HE FIRST SUNDAY OF LENT, ONCE OBSERVED BY the Western church as the first *day* of Lent, is historically known as "Quadragesima Sunday" because it takes place exactly forty days before Good Friday. This length of forty days for the Lenten fast symbolically aligns Lent with biblical examples of fasts and periods of preparation. For that reason, the church has preserved the forty-day duration even when making slight adjustments to the Lenten calendar over the centuries. For example, when both the Eastern and Western churches decided that Sundays should not count toward the forty days, they moved the start of Lent to slightly earlier—Clean Monday and Ash Wednesday, respectively—to make up for this change. The Eastern Church, because it begins earlier, counts only up until Holy Week (or Great Week), which is set aside as a separate fast.

This adjustment to the Lenten calendar reflects the church's consistent effort over the centuries to make room for feasting and celebration even within seasons of fasting. In the liturgical calendar, the church sees Sunday as a weekly microcosm of Easter—a day for celebrating the Resurrection. This is epitomized in the Eucharist, the *feast* of Holy Communion. But in addition to the theological reasons for the Sunday reprieve, the church recognizes the practical, human need for sustenance and encouragement in the midst of Lent. Sundays keep us from falling into a rut of fasting simply for the sake of self-denial; they remind us that the purpose of Lent is to prepare us to receive reconciliation and new life. The Lenten fast is always directed toward that promise of fulfillment, the promise that our hunger will be satisfied.

With these spiritual purposes of fasting in mind, then, the church extends the character of Lent into communal worship. While the fast is typically relaxed on Sundays, the sights and sounds of the liturgy are nevertheless stripped to a minimum. Clergy trade in the bright green vestments of Ordinary Time for robes of purple, the traditional color of repentance and humility. Flowers that usually decorate the altar are absent, and images throughout the church are veiled or removed, especially during Holy Week.

The sounds of worship are toned down as well; some churches stop using the organ during Lent and eliminate the more joyful recitations from the liturgy. Catholic and Episcopal churches, for example, omit the "Gloria in Excelsis" hymn and the "Alleluia" proclamation from worship. The word "alleluia" (meaning "praise the Lord") was initially adopted from Jewish tradition for special use in Easter worship. Gradually the Alleluia became a year-round presence in the liturgy, so that when it is removed from worship during Lent now, it is felt as a solemn absence. Some churches represent this removal ceremonially by carrying an alleluia banner or scroll out of the church on Ash Wednesday. The word is then brought back into the church—and the liturgy—during the Easter vigil. As with other joyful aspects of the liturgy that are temporarily suppressed during Lent, this declaration of celebration and praise disappears for a while, only to remind us of its great power when it is finally restored.

Richard John Neuhaus

SCRIPTURE
Psalm 63:1–11, 98, 103;
Deuteronomy 8: 1–10;
1 Corinthians 1:17–31;
Mark 2:18–22

Today's READINGS ARE BOTH CENTRAL AND compelling, and rightly used to start off the first Sunday of the Lenten season. We have the temptation scene of Adam and Eve and the temptation scene of Jesus, with two clear messages about how to deal with temptation.

But they do deserve a bit of explanation, and to be honest they deserve far more than I can possible give here. But I hope what little I do say will encourage you to some fruitful scripture study of your own.

Among the many things worth nothing in our Genesis reading (2:4–9, 15–17, 25–3:7) is that the result of Adam and Eve's seeming transgression is personal shame. They first note their own nakedness and sew fig leaves together to cover their new sense of separateness and suspicion.

They have "taken sides," as it were, against themselves and therefore apart from one another. Note that the "sin" involved does not really sound like a sin at all: eating of the tree of the knowledge of good and evil. Why would that be bad? It sounds like a good thing to me, but when your arrogance presumes that you totally and certainly know perfect good and perfect evil, "you will surely die." You have placed yourself in the position of God, and this is the first stern warning against all false moralizing and judging, and all cheap religion.

It separates us into our minds, out of our hearts and bodies (nakedness?), and apart from one another—and finally all of reality. The insight is pure religious genius, and if any part of the Bible is inspired it is surely this creation account (if you interpret it with wisdom).

In the Gospel we have Jesus playing the role of the corporate personality, or stand-in, for all of humanity, which was a common assumption in early New Testament theology. Here at the age of thirty he is the archetypal adult first moving into the world of power and influence. He symbolically (and I am sure truly) faces temptations to the misuse of power, temptations that we all must defeat if we are to use our adult power wisely and with holiness.

The misuse of our power, or failure to use our power at all, is what undoes most human lives. Jesus does neither here, but shows us a way through.

The three temptations here in Matthew are the universal temptations to three abuses of power: 1) the misuse of social or cultural power (turning stones into bread in a way that would be spectacular and draw attention to himself); 2) the misuse of religious power (to stand on the parapet of the temple and to quote scripture for his own purposes); 3) the misuse of political or dominative power (looking down on all the kingdoms of this world from a high mountain position).

The brilliant use of symbol here is totally effective for those who know that religion can *only* use metaphor to describe what are inherently spiritual realities. For those who do not respect this compelling and truthful use of metaphor, the message is normally missed or at least seriously lessened. Mere literalism is the lowest level of meaning, and that is surely true in both readings we have here today. Hold out for the big and always true meanings.

Note that in each case, Jesus merely uses scripture to expose and exorcise the demon, and all the demon can do is depart. Jesus does own his legitimate place and power, and yet very delicately he does not overidentify with this power, which would only set "an equal and opposite reaction" against him personally, but he deflects the energy from himself and quotes three very God-centered scriptures to show where the conflict finally lies—between God and evil and not between "me" and evil.

We make this mistake when our own ego gets involved, when we take things personally and fight back to defend our small insecure selves. This is perhaps the mistake that Adam and Eve made in regard to their temptation, which only put them in a state of greater exposure, nakedness, and shame. Jesus is shown here to be the ideal model of how to deal with temptation and how to recognize what the underlying temptation usually is—to a misuse or non-use of our very real human power. He refuses to eat of the tree of the knowledge of good and evil in any self-serving way, and leaves that final and full knowledge to God alone.

All powerful God, you have aligned yourself with powerlessness in our crucified Lord Jesus, and yet you and he are one. Show us how to hold power in the Father, hold powerlessness through the Son, and share and honor both of them in the Holy Spirit. Amen.

SCRIPTURE
Psalm 41, 44, 52;
Deuteronomy 8:11–20;
Hebrews 2:11–18;
John 2:1–12

THE READINGS FOR THIS WEEK WEAVE STRANDS from three biblical texts. The book of Deuteronomy ("Second Law") was another "copy" of the law that was first revealed in Exodus, Numbers, and Leviticus, but now with some new interpretations and emphasis. It has many beautiful and even poetic sections to it, and this particular week gives us what is called "the second discourse of Moses" where he sets forth the basic principles of the Law. You will see that it is not legalistic at all, but highly spiritual and eloquent.

The Letter to the Hebrews is not directly by Saint Paul according to most contemporary scholars, since it represents a completely different style, vocabulary, and set of themes. It is written to Jewish Christians, who have moved away from Jerusalem, in the "diaspora," as it is called, and they are nostalgically longing to return to what they are familiar with.

So the author makes use of metaphors and images that only a Jew would understand (temple, high priest, sacrifices, atonement), and tries to show how these all have been transmitted to Christ and transformed by Christ—so they do not need the temple anymore.

The Gospel of John is used generously in this lectionary. Our particular section for this week will inaugurate some of his central themes of "signs" and enlightenment.

With that as background, let's look at today's specific readings. Today's segment from Deuteronomy contains one of my favorite verses, which continues throughout the scriptures and finally becomes the full blown theme of grace in Paul's New Testament letters: "Beware of saying in your heart, 'My own strength and the might of my own hand has won this power for me.' Remember, Yahweh your God: it was he who gave you this strength and won you this power for me." This is a reminder to the Jewish people to remember that it is all a gratuitous gift from God.

This theme of remembrance of the *mirabilia Dei,* the wonderful works of God, even after we have grown comfortable and prosperous, becomes another constant theme in Jewish theology, and is introduced early here.

Our section from Hebrews is one of the clearest Biblical references to what my own Franciscan tradition would later call "the univocity of being," or what we would today call the circle of life. In other words, there is a unity between the Being of God and other beings. The author says, "The one who sanctifies, and the ones who are sanctified, are of the same stock ("of a single whole"). That is why [Jesus] openly calls them brothers [and sisters]."

My spiritual father, Francis, of course broadened this beyond the human and even called elements and animals "brother" and "sister" in his famous "Canticle of Brother Sun."

Finally, our Gospel reading from John is the lovely account of the wedding feast at Cana, found nowhere else. If nothing else, apart from showing that Jesus went to parties, apparently drank wine, and multiplied it for others, the text says that discipleship with Jesus is revealed as a wedding banquet more than some new legislation. "The best wine has been kept until now," and seemingly is given only if we really want it and ask for it. God is a good host and does not force our attendance or our enjoyment at the banquet of life. Jesus surely invites us to a world of abundance, companionship, and joy.

> You have set before us a banquet of life and love, good God. Why is that too good to believe? Why is it even too hard to enjoy or imagine? You have promised us a gratuitous love and even called us brother and sister in your Son, Jesus. Prepare us to celebrate this feast by a life of generosity and joy. Teach us the way of love instead of the way of fear. Amen.

SCRIPTURE
Psalm 45, 47, 48;
Deuteronomy 9:4–12;
Hebrews 3:1–11;
John 2:13–22

I N TODAY'S FIRST READING FROM DEUTERONOMY we have the verse that apparently inspired Jesus himself to do his fast in the desert, which then in turn became our forty days of Lent. Moses says to the rebellious Israelites, "I stayed forty days and forty nights on the mountain, with nothing to eat or drink."

A sacred pattern of time is being revealed, and forty is the consistent symbolic number. (Some think it was the average age of a person's life and so symbolized life and death itself.) This is also the time that Moses spent in the cloud on the mountaintop, and it was the duration of the great flood of Noah. It is eventually extended to the full forty years of wandering in the desert.

What's the significance of this number? Probably the way we would say it is: Trust the process, it's not over until it's over. "Forty days and forty nights" has become a mantra for all sacred time: time of temptation, time of ecstasy, and time of trial.

The first part of this same reading beautifully enunciates the growing theme of grace, again repeating "It is not for any goodness of yours that I am doing this." This new land of gratuitous divine love is the real promised land—a land we are all entering in fits and starts, just as the first Jews did.

This is a process quite different from any meritocracy, but it is hard for us to shake that mindset—we are all hesitant to leave the familiar world of earning and achieving to enter a world of freedom and gift.

Then our author in Hebrews continues to develop his understanding of Jesus as the new and "real" Moses, saying to his Christian Jews that Moses was faithful as a servant in his house, but Jesus is faithful as a son and the master of the house. To live in this house is to be confident with "a confidence that we can glory in" because we are sisters and brothers in the very same house.

This is much of his message to an exiled people who are neither confident nor at rest in their exile from home base in Judea. Surely they are a stand-in for all of us. These Christian Hebrews are quite normal people who hanker for the consolations of their early childhood religion, and so this Christian apologist is making his best case for it all being fulfilled in Christ and in the eternal house of God, as opposed to a mere temple in Jerusalem.

This all leads up rather perfectly to our Gospel today, where Jesus makes a whip of cords to do an act of religious protest that forever stands as a validation of the rituals of "civil disobedience." He symbolically replaces the temple with "the temple of his body," as not just more important than this sacred building, but its rightful and actual successor.

The human, the personal, the physical has become the new sacred. Anything which denies the true sacred is to be "driven out." Paul, the first theologian of Jesus, will take up this same meaning and metaphor when he frequently describes our human bodies as "temples" of God and the Holy Spirit. The human mind of Jesus somehow knew that he was the archetype and avatar of this mystery of divine incarnation, which is still the trump card of Christian belief.

The temple is forever personal and living and now.

Jesus knew that religion itself would constantly be tempted to substitute the means for the end, the medium for the message, the container for the actual contents. Religion always risks making God into a commodity that it could personally buy and sell, "turning my Father's house into a marketplace," as it were. It is without doubt his strongest act of public anger and an act of social resistance at the very center of Jewish economic and religious power. Many would say this was the action that clinched his fate. All we can conclude is that the message here is quite central and important for the very nature of religion and the search for God.

In one day of Lenten scriptures we have moved from sacred time (the symbolic number forty), to sacred relationship (brothers and sisters in God's household), to sacred space (the universal Body of Christ).

Our world is surely being rebuilt and refashioned.

You alone are good, you alone are sacred and holy, loving God, yet you have chosen to invite us into this promised land, into this household of God, into the temple that is your body, where we are not yet fully at home. Show us how to live here with conscious gratitude and confidence. We know it is your gift, but we still do not know how to receive free gifts. Amen.

SCRIPTURE
Psalm 49, 53, 119:49–72;
Deuteronomy 9:13–21;
Hebrews 3:12–19;
John 2:23–3:15

I N TRADITIONAL CHRISTIAN THEOLOGY IT IS impossible or even absurd for God to be upset or angry or vengeful, but we surely have a furious Yahweh in today's passage from Deuteronomy. He is angry at the "headstrong" Jewish people on their journey through the desert and at Aaron the priest for building the golden calf. Yahweh threatens to destroy them and "blot out their name from under heaven."

This sets some problems in motion.

Soon Moses joins in God's anger and destroys the stone tablets of the commandments and burns the golden calf, grinding it into fine dust. That is the trouble with such an anthropomorphic image of God. If your God is named as angry and punitive, you are soon legitimated in your own small-mindedness—without a whit of doubt that your rage is God's rage, too. This has been a major problem in much of the history of religion and has laid a basis for very punitive and even torturing Christianity.

But the text still has a narrative with much to teach. So let's just move beyond.

In the second reading from Hebrews, the key word is clearly *rest*. Between today and tomorrow's short entry it will be used ten times. The author has found how to rest, and it has something to do with living in the present moment. He or she beautifully conflates past, present, and future into a Biblical statement that later generations will call "the eternal now": "Everyday, as long as this 'today' lasts, keep encouraging one another"—in other words, keep being positive and loving no matter what.

I am not sure which comes first. Does loving keep you in the now or does living in the now allow you to love? They are both true, I think, and you can start on either side.

The only way that we can rest at peace in our minds is when we live in the fullness of the now, or what some in the Christian tradition called "the sacrament of the present moment." Otherwise life is just endlessly rehashing the past and rehearsing the future, neither of which create rest.

I always say that our common phrase "peace of mind" is an oxymoron. When you are at peace, you are never in your mind, and when you are in your mind, you are never at peace. The author also repeats the lovely word "confidence," but now says it even better: "Keep a grasp on your first confidence right to the very end." He says that this alone has the power to keep you from "hardness of heart" and rebellion.

In moments of hurt or discouragement, I often think of my early idealistic and youthful faith and how it seemed I could surmount almost anything with my seemingly simplistic "trust in the Lord." That was my first confidence, the early faith of the trusting child, that we often need to return to in times of later confusion and mental anxiety.

Then in our Gospel we have the momentous conversation between Jesus and Nicodemus in John 3:1–15. This passage has created a frame for centuries of talk about enlightenment, rebirth, the nature of spirit and flesh, our incapacity to ever control or dole out the Holy Spirit (which is like the wind), the fear and doubt of the sincere religious seeker.

This Gospel is a theological gold mine, and all I can do is offer you these brief allusions, in hopes that you will follow up on the ones that most intrigue you.

From the dangers of an anthropomorphic god created in our mind, to the meaning of true peace of mind, and then to a mind-blowing set of revelations, today's scriptures are made to order to give you a new mind, which Paul dares to call "the mind of Christ."

Jesus, you told us that we should love God with our mind, our heart, our body, and our soul. Show us how they can work as one, and how we can love all things not just in our heads, but with our heart, soul, and body too. Maybe that is how we can live with you in every eternal now. Teach us how to live in the present, because that might just teach us all we need to know. Amen.

SCRIPTURE

Psalm 19, 46, 50, 59, 60;
Deuteronomy 9:23–10:5;
Hebrews 4:1–10;
John 3:16–21

I MUST SAY THAT I LOVE THIS REPRESENTATIVE passage from Deuteronomy because it reveals two extraordinary things that are not found in the Scriptures of most religions. First, it shows an amazing capacity for self-criticism, which will evolve into the full "prophetic imagination," as Walter Brueggemann calls it. "Take no notice of this people's stubbornness, their wickedness, and their sin," Moses says. This continuing capacity for self-criticism is the absolute genius of the Hebrew tradition and scriptures, found nowhere else so clearly, except in Jesus himself (who was a Jew). Lack of honest self-criticism has been the tragic failure of all world religions, including all three of the monotheistic religions to this day.

Secondly, it reveals an almost humorous, but honest, relationship of a spiritual leader to his people, or for that matter many parents to their children. "They are *your* people and *your* inheritance!" Moses says defiantly to Yahweh. "You brought them to this peoplehood and dignity, now it is your responsibility to lead them from here. I don't know how to do it!" he seems to say. That is surely the clear implication of the text here and elsewhere.

Then in Hebrews we continue the wonderful theme of rest, used eight times in this passage. I am also told that this verb is the most common verb used in the Christian mystics. We are into something universal and archetypal here. There is a deep and constant desire for a place of rest in human nature. It is almost as if we know this life of climbing, competing, and contending is not our natural or desired mode.

Rest had become a description of the Promised Land for the Jewish wanderers, and further became symbolized in the very notion of the seventh day or Sabbath rest. No other religion has ever made non-performance such a clear article of faith as have the Jewish people. It was their own early and deep intuition about the need for a contemplative mind. At least one seventh of life must be non-working, non-achieving, and non-performing, or we do not know the depth, meaning, and joy of the other six days. A wonderful insight, even if both Jews and Christians have often interpreted it in legalistic and limited ways.

These two themes are brought together by our passage from John about God's relationship to "the world." It is all good news. "God sent not his Son into the world to condemn the world; but that the world through him might be saved." Clearly the word "world" referred to here is not bad, as later history often made it, but something that God loves and relates to.

The next important point in this passage is that the world is on trial before the brilliance of Jesus's life and judgment. His life cuts a clear line between what is real and what is unreal. His judgment is not external and punitive, but inherent and unfolding.

Our actions have "already" judged us. All punishments and rewards are inherent to reality itself. God does not need to judge afterward. Goodness is its own reward and evil is its own punishment: "On these grounds is sentence pronounced. . . . People have shown that they prefer darkness to light . . . every-body who does wrong hates the light and avoids it . . . but the person who does the truth comes into the light." Good people love goodness, even if they fail at it; evil people actually love evil and disrespect goodness unless it is some-thing they can manipulate and use for themselves.

Darkness and light here are not equated with joining any group or believing any doctrines, but *doing* the truth and *doing* the untruth. Yes, Jesus is the name of the one who does the truth, and if you love the truth you will naturally love him, as so many non-Christians in history have recognized. As Simone Weil put it, "Christ likes us to prefer truth to himself, because before being Christ, he is truth. If one turns aside from him to go toward the truth, one will not go far before falling into his arms."

> God of all truth, you are truth itself, and therefore truth is not an idea or a concept, but first of all a life, an energy, a love, a relationship with everything. Teach us to love truth and to truthfully love; then we always know we will be loving you. Amen.

SCRIPTURE
Psalm 40, 51, 54, 95;
Deuteronomy 10:12–22;
Hebrews 4:11–16;
John 3:22–36

THE SUCCESSIVE PASSAGES IN THE SAME THREE books continue to be rich. Today, we hear the entire worldview of Deuteronomy, where the possibility of love of God with whole heart and soul is perhaps first spoken of. In what would still be an early-stage and presumably externalized religion, we already have the author speaking of interiority, or "circumcision of the heart," and then equating conversion itself with what the Catholic tradition would now call "the corporal works of mercy." To do justice "for the orphan and widow" (outside the family social security system) and to "love the stranger, because you were yourself strangers in the land of Egypt" (outside the ethnic security system) show a finely developed ethic seven hundred years before Christ. Issues of intention and higher motivation are already being called forth.

Our passage ends by affirming that the promise to Abraham has thus already been fulfilled in their lifetime. It is not a future promise but a present reality: "God has made you as numerous as the stars of heaven."

Then we move to Hebrews for another poetic passage, an oft-quoted one about the word of God and its power to open up the interior self. It is one of the first places where soul is distinguished from spirit, soul being that which "joins" parts together, and spirit being the "marrow" of the message. Anyone trying to combine good therapy with good spiritual direction and "judge the secret emotions and thoughts" of the heart would love this passage. Scholars are not sure if the author first means the written word of God in the Scriptures or the personified word of God in Jesus, probably he or she wants to say that both of them—the scriptures and the risen Jesus—are "alive and active" agents that have the power of a "double-edged sword," or maybe the two edges are precisely the informational and the personal combined, which is surely the best and most convicting form of transformation.

Finally, we have a most interesting passage in John where Jesus is now revealed to also be "baptizing" and has clearly appropriated John's ritual as his own now. Remember that this was an offbeat ritual that would not have been condoned or even understood by the scribes or temple establishment—or John's own priestly family.

Spirit and mercy have become as accessible and available as river water, and outside the temple system. It is totally clear in the law who takes care of all purifications and atonements, and now both John and Jesus are creating a "para-church" situation. But John says clearly that they "only lay claim because it was given from above." He is not a rebel, but is himself obedient to a higher obedience. But how do we know that in the moment?

We must be honest and admit that this is quite daring and seemingly individualistic theology that most of us would likely mistrust if we were on site, but John sincerely plays the humble card to show he is not seeking to be a competing authority, but is only the friend of the bridegroom who feels joy at the bridegroom's voice and is quite happy to exit stage right as "he must grow greater and I must grow smaller." He is not ambitious, but is only seeking God's reign.

The Baptist justifies Jesus's appropriation of the river ritual by declaring proudly that "the Father loves the Son and has entrusted everything to his hands." Jesus is here to take religion to its organic next stage, not to rebel against its past. Then John adds that to trust this sonship (and by implication *your* own daughterhood or sonship) is to have eternal life now—present tense.

This is not about a later reward system. The interior and transformative journey that the first two readings point toward—the awakening of soul, the circumcision of heart, the baptizing of body, the release of Spirit—has now met its mark in this world. The economy of this world has become an economy of grace, and both John and Jesus are here to wash away any remnants of merit, atonement, or animal sacrifice.

The bridegroom is instead inaugurating a wedding feast.

> Lord of the Dance, Host of the Feast, free us to enter and enjoy the new heart and mind that you always offer humanity. Free us from all those things which make us small, smug, or superficial. Show us, by going first, how to dip under the waters of grace and mercy, and to never hold you to what we think you have said, if it holds us back from what you still want to say. Amen.

SCRIPTURE

Psalm 55, 138, 139:1–23;
Deuteronomy 11:18–28;
Hebrews 5:1–10;
John 4:1–26

Today we have the conclusion of Moses's discourse to his people. The words are grand and sweeping, and place the Jewish people at the center of history, and of their own lives, as all sacred scriptures must do. We have to feel special before we can tell others that they are special too. Chosen people pass on the gift, as we will soon see in the Gospel. The first verses today in Deuteronomy, however, are the lovely validation of what became Jewish phylacteries and mezuzahs. "Fasten these words on your hand and on your forehead!" "Write them on the doorpost of your house!" The Jewish people recognized the power of body marking, tactile daily reminders, and rituals to communicate deep and important truths.

Then Moses sets the standard for classic prophetic utterance by setting a clear dualistic choice before them: blessing or curse, life or death. No third way is possible. This pattern of clear choice and decision will be imitated by all later prophets and by Jesus himself. We called it a "fundamental option" in moral theology. Now the rest of the Bible will try to clarify for us two foundational questions that need much prayer and subtlety after we have made our fundamental option: "What then is life?" and "What is death?"

In our reading from Hebrews we have an important marker in trying to answer those questions. The author is trying to communicate to Jewish Christians that Jesus is still carrying the archetype of the high priest, but now in a very new form of solidarity and sympathy, as opposed to lineage, Levitical priesthood, or ordination. "He can sympathize with those who are ignorant or uncertain because he too lives in the limitations of weakness."

This is an altogether extraordinary statement, and one that deserves much prayer and commentary. He says that Jesus learned this obedience through suffering. We now have an utterly new kind of ordination, not one by appointment but one given by a different kind of seminary and actual life journey. It is the authority of those who have suffered—and lived to talk about it in a resurrected way.

This is the true ordination that transforms other people and the priest or minister himself. That this is a meaning intended is rather clear because he dredges up a completely obscure figure called Melchizedek, mentioned only in two short places in the Hebrew scriptures. Melchizedek was outside of any line of official priesthood, and just appeared on the scene "with bread and wine" but surely not part of any official line of priesthood. "The order of Melchizedek" is on a different plane than formal priestly lineage, but one who blesses out of his own inner authority and experience. Archetypal priesthood or ministry is not always the same as ordained ministry, and in Melchizedek we have one "bringing bread and wine" to bless Abram— seemingly out of nowhere.

This all leads up to Jesus engaging privately and yet publicly in a sustained conversation with a woman who is a foreigner and a formal sinner, risking scandal, and even putting himself in a needy and receiving position, all of which would have been quite unusual for a male in this time. He soon relativizes both her religion and his own in favor of a "worship in spirit and truth," which would have pleased nobody, and probably still doesn't. He reveals her humiliating personal secrets to her, but without humiliating her. They both keep talking and he also remains vulnerable and self-revealing, all leading up to a climactic and intimate "I am he." Any Christians who fear "commerce with the enemy" will not find much support from Jesus in this passage. Jesus is fully engaged and respectful, and even invitational.

"If you but knew the gift of God" seems to be Jesus' primary message here, but he presents it in a reciprocal way. He asks her for a drink of water and then moves the conversation to symbolic "living water," and then says that this gift will turn into a spring inside her. The gift that Jesus gives and that Jesus is—is given, received, and now fully possessed by her and for her—and *as* her. The transformation is complete, purposeful, and joyful.

This is the purpose of Lent.

God of Spirit and Truth, you give us truth so large that we know it has to be true everywhere, all the time, and for everybody—or it is not your truth. Give us hearts and minds that can stand humbly and patiently before such truth. May we fasten it on our doorposts, plant it in our hearts, and bring the blessings of your bread and wine, and your living water, to a hungry world. Amen.

SECOND WEEK OF
LENT

H ISTORICALLY, THE SEASON OF LENT HAS HAD two distinct but related purposes: penance and the preparation for baptism. Of the two, the penitential character of Lent is more familiar to us today. The Lenten liturgy emphasizes repentance with dark liturgical colors, minimized music, and readings and prayers that stress confession and a return to God. Weekday services in the Orthodox Church feature an increased amount of bowing and prostration—physical postures meant to express humility and repentance.

The penitential character of Lent was evident in an early-church practice of reconciliation designed for Christians whose grievous sins had caused them to be excluded from the church. These penitents were invited to public confession at the start of Lent and would follow prescribed acts of penance throughout the weeks leading up to Easter, when they would be joyfully received back into the church. Gradually, this practice became a more generalized invitation to all Christians to prepare themselves for Easter through self-examination and repentance.

Two important penitential practices still associated with Lent are fasting—going without food or drink for a designated period of time—and the related practice of abstaining from particular kinds of food. The early church adopted fasting and abstinence from Jewish custom and from the example of Jesus, seeing these practices as aids to mindfulness, prayer, and receptivity to God.

Today, most Christians who observe Lent abstain from meat on Fridays; some traditions also call for a full fast on Ash Wednesday and Good Friday. Orthodox believers abstain not only from meat but also eggs, fish, olive oil, alcohol, and dairy products throughout the duration of Lent (often excepting Saturdays and Sundays).

In addition to fasting in this way, many Christians choose to give up something, such as a favorite food or activity, for Lent. These optional fasts became popular in the twentieth century after the Catholic Church relaxed its more rigorous fasting requirements, and are embraced today by Orthodox, Protestants, and Catholics alike as a way to cultivate the practice of restraint and help believers to reduce distractions and depend more fully on God.

The elimination of meat and other items from the Lenten diet has resulted in a variety of creative Lenten traditions. Eastern Europeans serve mushroom or vegetable pies instead of meat pies throughout the season. Fish became popular on meatless Fridays after being deemed an acceptable Lenten cuisine in the West, and Friday "fish fries" and Lenten soup dinners bring many American churchgoers together throughout Lent. The presence of small feasts like these suggest that Lent is best understood as a time not of denial for its own sake, but for *redirecting* our desires toward that which nourishes us both spiritually and physically, preparing us for fuller communion with God and each other.

In Christian theology, repentance is understood to encompass not only sorrow for sin but also the need for a positive change, a *turn toward* God. As a complement to Lenten fasting, then, Christians often add devotional practices to their daily lives, such as prayer, scripture reading, or attending special church services throughout the week. Lenten observance also traditionally includes an emphasis on charity and almsgiving; many churches organize opportunities for serving the poor during Lent, inviting congregants to extend their more personal acts of repentance and growth to the service of the greater community.

Lauren F. Winner

Second Sunday of Lent

SCRIPTURE
Psalm 8, 24, 29, 84;
Jeremiah 1:1–10;
1 Corinthians 3:11–23;
Mark 3:31–4:9

God IS A STORM. THAT IS WHAT LEAPS OUT AT ME from the psalmist's imagery: God's stormy thundering voice breaks the cedars.

During the rest of the week, we will be encountering images in the Psalms of God as a *refuge* from the storms. Those are more appealing images. I prefer them to images of God's storminess.

Yet, somehow both are true. God is a refuge from the storm, and God is the storm.

I'd rather skip the stormy images altogether. But Lent is an apt time to encounter the psalmist's insistence on the God who is not just a harbor, but also a storm.

For Lent is a journey into unprotectedness. Lent is being willing to expose ourselves to storminess. Jesus moves from seeming unprotectedness in the wilderness to utter vulnerability on the cross. And Lent is an opportunity to ask how much energy we pour into protecting ourselves—from the storms we encounter on the path to true self-knowledge, from the storms we encounter when we genuinely love our neighbor, from the storms that are God, and the storms that God protects us from.

During Lent, I often reread one of my favorite passages from all of American fiction, a passage from Jane Smiley's novella

The Age of Grief. It is narrated by a middle-aged man who has intuited that his wife is having an affair. He spends the entire novella trying to prevent his wife from actually telling him of this affair, but at the very end of the novella she does finally speak of it—and shortly before that happens, the narrator has this rumination:

> I am thirty-five years old, and it seems to me that I have reached the age of grief. Others arrive there sooner. Almost no one arrives much later. I don't think it is the years themselves, or the disintegration of the body.... What it is, is what we know, now that in spite of ourselves we have stopped to think about it.... It is not only that, by this time, a lot of acquaintances and friends have died and all the others are getting ready to sooner or later. It is more that the barriers between the circumstances of oneself and the rest of the world have broken down, after all...the cup must come around, cannot pass from you, and it is the same cup of pain that every mortal drinks from.

That the barriers between the circumstances of oneself and the rest of the world might break down: that is one of the invitations of Lent. That the barriers between me and God might break down. If I approach Lent with a genuine desire to follow Jesus into the wilderness, it will be a season in which God's voice may break some of the cedars in my own backyard.

It will be a season of storms, some of which God will protect me from, some of which God will provoke—and in all of that, God will be present.

O Lord God, who sees that we put not our trust in any thing that we do, mercifully grant that by your power we may be defended against all adversity; through Jesus Christ our Lord. Amen. (Book of Common Prayer)

Second Monday of Lent

SCRIPTURE
Psalm 56, 57, 58, 64, 65;
Jeremiah 1:11–19;
Romans 1:1–15;
John 4:27–42

O H, THE WOMAN BY THE WELL! OF ALL THE characters in Scripture, her faith story—if that is a fair way to describe what we read in the fourth chapter of the Gospel of John—is one to which I especially relate and one to which I most aspire.

The woman has this encounter by Jesus at the well, and, though she is not totally clear about what just happened ("Could this be the Messiah?" she asks with a little hesitation, a little uncertainty), she knows it was important. She is so eager to tell her neighbors about the man she just met that she leaves behind her water jug.

What makes her feel such urgency? Is it too simple to suggest that she encountered God's forgiveness—and that an encounter with God's forgiveness does, indeed, inspire urgent feelings? *I just experienced something amazing. I have to tell someone. I'm not even totally sure what the experience was, I just know it was—everything.*

Forgiveness: on this story's terms, forgiveness is God's love for us, given all God knows.

God looks at those things in my life that I find most shameful. God looks at my most secret sins, the things that make me curdle. God looks at them and God sees something to love.

Yes, of course, God also calls for my amendment of life. God thunders through the prophets in all these stern and uncomfortable Lenten readings about how far off I am. God wants to stir up some awareness in me—God wants me to notice, and care, that I have wandered off (or perhaps not wandered—perhaps I marched). God wants me to change, to return.

And yet God desires us to return precisely because God looks at us and loves us, never mind all God knows about our secret shames. God wants to keep company with us, even so.

I was recently a guest at a wedding where the pastor stood, smiling and beckoning, as two very young flower girls toddled down the aisle. The girls were often off course, veering, stopping halfway, getting distracted by a hat. And at the end of the aisle was the pastor, beckoning, smiling—and eventually, somehow, those two little flower girls made their way to her.

That pastor seemed to me like God.

God stands before us, beckoning us, still beckoning, even as we tarry and get distracted and meander, with our basket of rose petals, off course. God is beckoning to us.

God knew everything about that woman at the well—everything about her. And God beckoned her over regardless.

God wanted her to come to him. She sensed God's beckoning and it set her into action. She had just, perhaps for the first time ever, had the experience of all at once being known and loved. That is a rare experience—to be truly known, and loved all the same.

Who do you say that I am, Jesus asks us. He asks us over and over.

Here is one answer: he knows everything about me; he knows my most corrosive, hidden shame; and he beckons me toward him, nonetheless.

> Living Water...who...refreshes our weariness,
> bathes and washes and cleanses our wounds
> be for us always
> a fountain of life,
> and for all the world, a river of hope,
> springing up in the midst
> of the deserts of despair.
> Honor and blessing,
> glory and praise
> to you for ever and ever.
> Amen. (Medical Mission Sisters)

SCRIPTURE
Psalm 61, 62, 68:1–36;
Jeremiah 2:1–13;
Romans 1:16–25;
John 4:43–54

JEREMIAH 2:2: "I REMEMBER THE DEVOTION OF your youth, how as a bride you loved me and followed me through the wilderness."

At those words, I pause, and my mind and my prayers want to go in two directions. One direction leads to some place about my own individual spiritual life—some prayerful pondering about the difference between my young bridal love for God, back when I first became a Christian, and my undeniably less ardor-filled love now.

And that would be a fine set of devotional ponderings.

But my mind and my prayer ultimately tug in a different direction: instead of pondering my own lack of ardor, I find myself sitting with Jeremiah's metaphor—and its consequences.

The metaphor is a marriage: Israel is the wife, God the husband. Here in Jeremiah 2, we learn that the moment at Sinai was a moment of ultimate faithfulness, the moment at which Israel was that most devoted, thrilled wife.

And as we keep reading, we see that wife Israel would for years after be judged by that moment—and found wanting.

Twenty-nine chapters later, God will assert that God has loved Israel all along, everlastingly, and continued to be faithful throughout. But in the intervening chapters, there are lots of threats. Israel is a beloved young bride, then she is wayward and her husband threatens her, and eventually they are reunited, by the power of the husband's love. The wife has transgressed, but the husband has forgiven her, and their subsequent marriage will be all the more wonderful for his magnanimity.

Jeremiah is not the only place we find this metaphor. Ezekiel and Hosea, too, image Israel as a promiscuous wife, and depict God as a husband—an angry, violent husband. The texts, in the words of biblical scholar and pastor Renita Weems, "rationalize" and "eroticize" violence: "*God* is described as an *abusive husband* who batters his wife, strips her naked, and leaves her to be raped by her lovers, only to take her back in the end, insisting that when all is said and done, Israel the wife shall remain interminably the wife of an abusing husband...."

These descriptions, those images, have consequences. As Weems explains, "[T]he battered, promiscuous wife in the books of Hosea, Jeremiah, and Ezekiel makes rape, mutilation, and sexual humiliation defensible forms of retaliating against wives accused of sexual infidelity. Audiences are invited to imagine with the writers plausible ways of treating women."

I see the consequences every week in the spiritual autobiography classes and biblical interpretation classes I teach to women who have been abused by their husbands and brothers and uncles. Consequences indeed.

This is not really what I want to be thinking about during my devotional time. I would much rather be following my more spiritual-sounding thoughts about the fading of my ardor. I don't really want to be thinking about this—but there it is, Jeremiah 2;

and shoving away the troubling pieces of the prophets' marital metaphor is not something I want to do either. It would not be fair to Denise, or to Sandy, or to the other women I teach. It would not be fair to the Bible. It would not be fair to God.

It is Lent: I want to ask God's forgiveness for the violence the church has countenanced, violence against women underwritten by these texts.

I want to ask God to protect and succor and heal the women who are being beaten right now, right this minute as I pray.

I want to ask God to help us change.

> God, we confess that, even in this faith community, many women, children and some men are abused.... We pledge our faith community to be a safe haven for those who are battered, a support for abusers sincerely seeking help, and an advocate for nonviolence in the world. Help us to be signs of your unconditional love in the world. Amen. (The Community of Our Lady for Perpetual Help, Salem, Virginia)

SCRIPTURE

Psalm 72, 119: 73–96;
Jeremiah 3:6–18;
Romans 1:28–2:11;
John 5:1–18

I CAN'T BELIEVE SHE SAID THAT."

"I can't *believe* he thought it was a good idea to show up at that party, so soon after..."

Those are words that have come out of my mouth—in the last three days.

Also: "I just don't understand why anyone would choose to live in this kind of subdivision, when they could have clearly bought a cool historic bungalow for the same money."

So...I can be a tad judgmental.

I strike the same note about more serious matters, too. I will watch a friend making unwise choices, and instead of sitting with my concern, I go to a place of judgment: "For crying out loud, she really should know better than..."

Sometimes the impulse to judge is my own insecurity, redirected. Some-times it is worry, misdirected, or a hurt feeling, misdirected. Sometimes it is just plain superiority and cattiness (see the comment about cool historic bungalows, above).

And here comes the apostle Paul: at whatever point you judge another, you are condemning yourself, because you who pass judgment do the same things. (Jesus occasionally struck a similar chord: *First remove the plank from your own eye; cast the first stone, etc.)*

Those words cut me to the quick. I am no less a sinner than any of the people I have spoken judgmentally of this week, or this year. I have made my own share of terrible decisions. (And, in the cattier matter of my passing judgment about the style of house someone wants to live in—well, to each her own.)

This Lent, I am trying to set aside my habit of judging other people. This does not mean I should stop holding any beliefs about right or wrong, of course. It does not mean I cannot try to help a friend see another way when I think she is doing something harmful, or sinful, or just plain stupid.

It does mean that I should try to cultivate compassion, instead of just criticizing. It does mean I should remember what Michael said to me just last month when I was off in the direction of "she really should know better." He said: "It is really hard to be a human being."

It is really hard to be a human being. That is what I am going to try to say to myself next time the bilious judgment rises up.

I have had these thoughts before—that I am too judgmental, that I really ought to stop. But it is interesting to encounter Paul's words, and have these thoughts, during Lent. For read in the season of Lent, my judgmental comments seem to be, among other things, one of those barriers between me and other people—and ultimately between me and true self-knowledge.

If I criticize you, I don't have to acknowledge the ways that we are the same, the ways I, too, have done foolish, sinful things. I push away knowledge of my own flaws and failings by setting myself above you and your flaws and failings. Lent is an invitation to stop.

Almighty ever living God, you are always more ready to hear than we to pray, and to give more than we desire or deserve; pour upon us the abundance of your mercy, forgiving us those things of which our conscience is afraid, and giving us those things for which our prayer dares not ask. Amen. (Book of Common Prayer)

Second Thursday of Lent

SCRIPTURE
Psalm 70, 71, 74;
Jeremiah 4:9–10, 19–28;
Romans 2:12–24;
John 5:19–29

THEREFORE THE EARTH WILL MOURN and the heavens above grow dark....

During Lent, we undertake special prayers and reading and fasts and disciplines, all designed to provoke in us a sense of mourning—mourning over sin.

The startling suggestion of those words from Jeremiah is that human beings and God are not the only ones who can thus mourn. Apparently all of creation is affected by, and can mourn over, sin.

Elsewhere in scripture, we are told of the planets and heavens singing God's praise:

The heavens declare the glory of God;
  the skies proclaim the work of his hands.
Day after day they pour forth speech;
  night after night they reveal knowledge.
They have no speech, they use no words;
  no sound is heard from them.
Yet their voice goes out into all the earth,
  their words to the ends of the world.

The heavens and skies and planets and stars praise—and mourn. And Lent may be the season when not just people enter into more intentional mourning; perhaps the earth is entering deeper into that mourning, too.

Or perhaps Lent is the season when we can most fully *notice* Earth's mourning. The Jesus we have followed into the wilderness, after all, came to redeem not just humanity, but all of creation. The consequences of the fall, the effects of sin, are written into the creation (and that ancient writing is compounded by the way human sin spills itself over the earth and the heavens, in the form of pollution, destructive carbon emissions, and a generally cavalier disregard for the imperative that we care for God's creation).

If the earth mourns, surely we, human beings, should be mourning also. An observation Laurie J. Braaten made about a passage from the Book of Joel is apt here, too: "Earth is suffering and mourns. Earth serves as a proper model for human mourning...should not readers identify with Earth's mourning?

Earth suffers violence—should not readers repent of the evil that made this happen? Readers pray for a transformed Earth—should not they depend on the mercy of God...to effect this change? In the meantime," Earth mourns.

The mourning is not just breast-beating and wailing, of course. It is not just morose; it is not just heavy. There is something light in mourning—or at least something lightening—precisely because there is something *true* in mourning.

To mourn the consequences of sin is, oddly, to edge very close to joy, because any encounter with the truth, even the truth of sin, has some hint of the lightened joy that comes when we allow ourselves to see things not as we wish they were, but as they really are; and a hint of the joy that will come when sin is no more.

And so this Lent I am walking through the landscape of my city, and I am walking by the Eno River, and I am walking through the botanical gardens attached to the university where I teach. And I am trying to allow the earth to teach me to mourn.

> God, you made the universe with all its marvelous order, its atoms, worlds, and galaxies, and the infinite complexity of living creatures: Grant that, as we probe the mysteries of your creation, we may come to know you more truly, and more surely fulfill our role in your eternal purpose. Amen. (Adapted from the Book of Common Prayer)

SCRIPTURE
Psalm 69:1–38, 73, 95;
Jeremiah 5:1–9;
Romans 2:2–3:18;
John 5:3–47

I WILL BE HONEST: WHEN NOT PROMPTED BY THE lectionary, I do not devote a lot of time to reading these prophetic denunciations of our sinful ways. I am sure I probably should read them of my own leisurely accord, but I don't.

They are uncomfortable. They discomfit. They tell me that: a) my wrongdoing matters to God and b) I have a chance to decide what I want to do about that wrongdoing. That would be non-disconcerting (indeed, it might even feel like good news) if, at "b," I always said "Hooray! I am so glad for the chance to do something different! I will stop the wrongdoing posthaste."

Since I do not always say that, the readings disconcert.

I find myself, sometimes, feeling very alone when I read Jeremiah (and John the Baptist, and even sometimes Jesus, who has a few harsh words about sinful ways). I think about my erring ways, and I feel very alone, very far away from God, very far away from a friend, close only to the sin.

Intellectually, I know this means I have progressed. Ten years ago, I didn't have any real awareness of my sin, let alone a feeling of compunction. In my head, I realize this very alone feeling might be a mark of growth in love of Christ, growth toward Christ, growth into Christlikeness.

But how it *feels* is alone.

So I will let the saints who have gone before remind me that I am not alone.

I have friends, I have a church, I have a pastor, and, above all, I have a friend in Jesus.

I will let the saints, those who have gone before and are now cheering me on my race, remind me that we are not alone in this journey into unprotectedness—we are doing this together, with one another—and we are doing it with Christ.

The poet George Herbert wrote a poem about Lent, and it tells us pretty well what at least one of the fruits of this season will be:

Who goeth in the way which Christ hath gone,
Is much more sure to meet him, than one,
That travelleth byways:
Perhaps my God, though he be far before,
may turn and take me by the hand and more,
May strengthen my decays.

My decays, says Herbert—God may strengthen my decays.

Decay of course means decline. Our bodies decay, and in early modern poetry decay can simply mean death. If you are a physicist, decay is the disintegration that happens to a nucleus.

Decay is also a springtime word; it is a gardening word: my gardening glossary tells me that compost is "The result and act of combining organic materials under controlled conditions so that the original raw ingredients are transformed by decay...into humus."

That is Lent: the transformation of our organic materials under controlled conditions so that our raw ingredients are transformed into humus—into life, into fertility.

It is a transformation we do together, as members of the same church family. It is a transformation we do with Jesus himself, who is even now turning, and extending us his hand.

> Who goeth in the way which Christ hath gone,
> Is much more sure to meet him, than one,
> That travelleth byways:
> Perhaps my God, though he be far before,
> may turn and take me by the hand and more,
> May strengthen my decays. Amen. (from George Herbert's "Lent")

Second Saturday of Lent

SCRIPTURE
Psalm 23, 27, 75,76;
Jeremiah 5:20–31;
Romans 3:19–31;
John 7:1–13

H ERE, IN THE THICK OF OUR CHRISTIAN SEASON of Lent, we read in out Gospel passage a mention of a Jewish holiday. Jesus, in the Gospel of John, is arguing with his brothers about whether he will celebrate Sukkot, the Festival of Huts, in Jerusalem.

It seems, at first, a little odd to be thinking about Sukkot during Lent. Jews celebrate Sukkot in the fall; it was celebrated some five or so months ago. Why am I thinking about a holiday that is half a year away?

But upon deeper pondering, it seems that Lent is a very fitting time to reflect on Sukkot.

Sukkot is celebrated as a weeklong holiday, and if, during that holiday, you walk past a synagogue, or past the home of an observant Jewish family, you might spy a sukkah, a hut.

Those huts are meant to imitate, and remind Jews of, the temporary dwellings in which the children of Israel lived during their forty years of wilderness wanderings. A sukkah has three walls and a roof; often the roof is made of branches, or corn husks; the roof is translucent; you have to leave enough space between those husks to see the stars. During the week of Sukkot, observant Jews take all their meals in the sukkah, they study there, and read, and sometimes sleep in their sukkah. So a sukkah usually holds a table, and a few sleeping bags.

It also holds the dance of vulnerability and dependence, shelter and exposure; that is our relationship with God.

Sukkot not only recalls the story of the Israelites in the wilderness, it teaches lessons about dependence and certainty. It teaches that security comes not from our houses or our jobs or our marriages or our ministries, but from God. It teaches that the things that appear most stable are flimsy, and the things that sometimes seem shaky are trustworthy. As the nineteenth-century German rabbi Samson Raphael Hirsch said: "The building of the [sukkah] teaches you trust in God.... You know that whether men live in huts or in palaces, it is only as pilgrims that they dwell; both huts and palaces form only our transitory home. You know that in this pilgrimage only God is our protection."

Those Sukkot words startle when we read them during Lent precisely because the God in whom we find our protection is the God of Good Friday. The God in whom we find our protection may have argued about going to Jerusalem for Sukkot, but he was the God who ultimately had his face set toward Jerusalem, and to the exposure and agony he would encounter there.

Our protection is a God who spurned protection. Our protection is a God of vulnerability.

And so we are back where we began a week ago, with the question of shelter.

The pledge of Lenten observance is this: we will be vulnerable as the children of Israel were vulnerable in the desert, and as God sheltered them, so might God shelter us.

We will be vulnerable as Christ was vulnerable, and it is in Christ himself where we will find our shelter.

> Assist us mercifully with thy help, O Lord God of our salvation; that we may enter with joy upon the meditation of those mighty acts, whereby thou hast given unto us life and immortality; through Jesus Christ our Lord. Amen. (Book of Common Prayer)

THIRD WEEK OF
LENT

MOST CHRISTIANS WHO OBSERVE LENT ARE familiar with the Lenten traditions of fasting and penance, but far fewer are familiar with Lent's origins as a time of baptismal preparation. From as early as the second century, the majority of converts to Christianity were being baptized at the Easter vigil on the night before Easter, a practice that was made official at the council of Nicaea in AD 325. For a period of time leading up to Easter (eventually the standard forty days), these baptismal candidates would perform acts of penance and self-examination in addition to fasting for one or two days before Easter.

Many of the penitential customs that we now associate with Lent probably grew out of this practice of baptismal preparation. By the sixth century, however, infant baptism had become the norm, and baptismal preparation was no longer so prevalent during Lent, since fewer adults were being baptized. The traditions of preparation once associated with Christian initiation became more generalized in the Christian community, and the church began to treat Lent as a time for all adults to prepare for Easter, the most important feast day of the church year.

Remembering Lent's historical connection with practices of Christian initiation and baptismal preparation can enrich our experience of Lent today. Just as new converts would use the weeks before Easter to learn the teachings of the church, so Christians today can take advantage of this season of minimized distraction to study the scriptures and teachings of their faith. Indeed, many Christian denominations still prefer to baptize new converts on Easter, so Lent naturally becomes a time for these kinds of preparations. On Sundays during Lent, the liturgy emphasizes preparation for inauguration into the Christian life with gospel and epistle readings that focus on repentance and the new life in store for believers. While Christ's Passion is a natural focus of the latter weeks of Lent, we might consider the early weeks of Lent as time to renew our faith as members of the Christian community.

In Orthodox Christianity, this division is actually built into Lent, with the first weeks focusing on individual fasting, preparation, and devotional exercises. Roughly halfway through Orthodox Lent, the third Sunday marks a turning point, shifting the focus from our individual sacrificial efforts to Christ's sacrifice on the cross. Orthodox Christians know the third Sunday of Lent as the Sunday of the Veneration of the Cross, or simply Holy Cross. The vigil of the Holy Cross features a procession of the cross, which is displayed for reverent contemplation. Going forward, this attention to the cross will continue to deepen with the approach of Holy Week. But as with Laetere Sunday in the Western tradition, Orthodox Christians see their mid-Lent Sunday as a time of refreshment and encouragement. When turning to the cross halfway through Lent, the faithful are reminded that, while Lenten efforts may have brought fatigue, ultimate deliverance does not depend on human strength: through the cross and Resurrection, Christ has already conquered sin and death.

Scott Cairns

SCRIPTURE

Psalm 34, 93, 96;
Jeremiah 6:9–15;
1 Corinthians 6:12–20;
Mark 5:1–20

T HE SUNDAY OF THE HOLY CROSS IS WHEN OUR
calendar encourages us to turn more intentionally onto
the road that will lead us to Christ's passion (see history of this
feast day). If we have been paying due attention to our journey
along the way, we will have confronted the so-far chronic
illness of our personal sin—our missing of the mark—will have
examined the untoward effects of that illness on our persons and
in our relationships with others; through prayer and fasting we
will have experienced some measure of what I think of as the ache
of repentance, which is the beginning of our healing

We also will have apprehended some sense of our own
insufficient strength, having felt the physical effects of fasting on
our bodies and its psychological effects upon our souls. That is
to say, at this point—not quite halfway through our journey—we
may well feel a little worn out, a little depressed. We may feel a
tad bit cranky.

Don't beat yourself up. This sense of having already met—and
so quickly—the limits of our strength is actually a very good thing.

Like the children of Israel, we already have traveled a
significant distance, have tasted the waters of the desert, and

have found them to be bitter. This is where the cross comes to our assistance.

As Moses dipped the wood into the bitter waters of *Marah* to make them sweet and life-sustaining, so, too, the wood of the Holy Cross is planted mid the waters of our desert passage, sweetening our portion as we—by its power—are now made able to move ahead.

Before my becoming Orthodox, this Lenten season didn't figure much into my thinking; it barely registered—not so much as a blip on my dim radar. Even after my chrismation, I must say that it took me a few years before I finally began to understand the efficacy of the Lenten fast; it took a good three years before I would come to know this somber period of preparation as a *blessing*.

That is to say, at first, I was surely among the crew that Father Alexander Schmemann acknowledges when he writes (in his amazing and very helpful book, *Great Lent*), "For many, if not for the majority of Orthodox Christians, Lent consists of a number of formal, predominantly negative, rules and prescriptions.... Such is the degree of our alienation from the real spirit of the Church that it is almost impossible for us to understand that there is 'something else' in Lent—something without which all these prescriptions lose much of their meaning."

Father Schmemann goes on to explain that this "something else" is another disposition altogether. He characterizes it as an "atmosphere," a "climate," and "a state of mind, soul, and spirit." In my own experience—which, as I say, required some years of practice before I so much as noticed—Lent can become an incentive and a powerful means by which we can enter the kingdom of God, even as we abide here on earth.

This disposition is the *harmolype*—the bright-sadness—of which the fathers and the mothers speak. Even in the dryness of our desert journey, we are offered a sustaining taste of the sweet, the living waters. Even amid the gloom, we apprehend a glimmer of the light.

Holy God, as we enter into another week of our slow preparation, anticipating your saving passion, we turn our eyes away from our own sore insufficiency and lift them to your Holy Cross. We seek all the more earnestly to relinquish our dim will to your illumination. We ask you to help us to shed our petty self-concern, our failed self-sufficiency. We ask for your uplifting care.

In Paradise, our ancient home, a tree once stripped us utterly of life; for by giving us its fruit to eat, the enemy fed us death, and we partook.

Today the Tree of thy most Holy Cross is raised upon the earth, filling all the world with joy and with thanksgiving, that we, partaking of its holy, life-giving fruit might once more be made whole, infused with your life.

We lift our living voices, praying: Glory to the Father, and to the Son, and to the Holy Spirit. Amen.

SCRIPTURE
Psalm 77, 79, 80;
Jeremiah 7:1–15;
Romans 4:1–12;
John 7:14–36

TODAY'S READINGS IN THE PSALMS ARE AMONG those that—in the past—I have found very difficult to speak aloud, laden as they are with lamentation for my sin, regret for my distance from God, and grief for the sorry, unhealthy state into which I have allowed God's temple—my person—to fall and to remain. As with most Psalms that speak of "heathens" and of "enemies," Psalm 79 is a text that remains open to a particularly efficacious and revelatory reading by which I may finally apprehend that these enemies are most profoundly the evil in my own heart.

In this way, I finally am able to realize that I am the one responsible for having opened the gate; I am the one who has invited the heathen to enter. I am the one who has colluded with the enemy, and the one most responsible for the fallen state of this temple that should be God's dwelling place, my heart.

In his letter to the Romans, Saint Paul insists that, like our father Abraham, we are in position to be accounted righteous, even so. Like Abraham, we might rise and walk in the steps of faith. Even that very first and tentative step of faith, regardless of our failures, will be "accounted to [us] as righteousness."

I recall a conversation that I was blessed to have with a saintly priest-monk during one of my first visits to Mount Athos in Greece. He was speaking of forgiveness, even as I was speaking to him of my own failures, and of how I was having trouble letting go of guilt and shame over past sins. It was then that Father Palamás pointed out to me that the one significant difference between Judas Iscariot and Saint Peter—both of whom had betrayed, had denied Christ—was that Peter believed he could be forgiven and Judas could not.

This modest and simple faith in our God's goodness—this faith in his exceeding *willingness* to forgive—is how we first begin to accept the great gift of repentance, trusting that we can be healed, made whole.

It is during the Feast of the Tabernacles that Christ quietly enters Jerusalem alone, having allowed his brothers to precede him; he enters the temple to teach. His teaching has very much to do with faithfulness and trust; he tells us how we might recognize a trustworthy witness. "Whoever speaks from himself seeks his own glory, but whoever seeks the glory of the one who sent him is true, and there is no unrighteousness in him."

As we continue our Lenten journey this day, let us keep our eyes upon the One Who sent the Christ, the same God—yesterday, today, and forever—who now sends us. Let us give our most strenuous attention to the preparation of his tabernacle, our very bodies; let us ask for his cleansing of the temple; hereafter, let us ask his help in our remaining watchful as we guard the gate.

Loving God, you know that repeatedly I have opened to the enemy the gates of my heart, your holy tabernacle. I have made of your house an impure dwelling. With your loving care, enter this temple now, assist me in rooting out all that is unclean, cleanse this wound, and help me to recover the beauty of your house, remaining watchful, alert to everything that would threaten our developing communion. For you alone are the lover of mankind, Father, Son, and Holy Spirit. Amen.

Third Tuesday of Lent

SCRIPTURE
Psalm 78;
Jeremiah 7:21–34;
Romans 4:13–25;
John 7:37–52

IN ORDER FOR US TO WITNESS ANY LASTING BENEFIT from the lessons of the past, we must take care to hear them, receive them, and—perhaps this is the most important step—*to speak them in turn* to our children.

I have an increasingly keen sense that our apprehension of any difficult matter is most available when we actually *speak* what we have heard. Just as a great poem opens up to us when we say it aloud, so too do we discover unexpected significance in *saying* what we think, in giving the bodily energies of breath and pulse and the resonance of our voices to our otherwise disembodied thoughts. In this way, we begin to *embody* our faith.

My own slow journey into prayer has been assisted by one essential teaching of the early church: that our faith is not simply a matter of propositions, nor of doctrines, nor of ideas, but is necessarily a matter of *incarnation*, of our embodying what we believe, performing that faith with our lives.

Much of the Lenten journey—the long and slow-moving services of the church, the dark vestments, and (most importantly) the coupling of prayer with fasting, and of fasting with almsgiving—has a way of quieting distractions and centering our minds within our hearts. These disciplines re-connect our minds to our bodies, assist our re-pairing our parsed and scattered persons into souls made whole; they also recover for us our often-overlooked connection with others.

The ancient tradition that teaches us to pray within this deep and heart-felt stillness—this tradition that assists us in seeing how our very lives might actually *become* prayer—begins with the advice that, before all else, we seek to quiet our busy thoughts. The fathers encourage this quieting, this stillness, in a number of ways, but I have found the following from Saint Isaak of Syria to be most helpful: "Enter eagerly into the treasure house that is within you, and you will see the things that are in heaven—for there is but one single entry to them both. The ladder that leads to the Kingdom is hidden within your soul. Dive into yourself, into your soul, and there you will find the ladder by which to ascend."

During Lent, the prayer of Saint Ephrem is recited twice near the end of each of our Orthodox weekday services. The prayer itself, of course, does a great deal to encourage within our hearts a penitential disposition, but that disposition is greatly enhanced by the bodily prostrations that accompany the prayer.

It is one thing to *think* of repentance, to turn our minds toward Christ and away from sin; it is an altogether greater thing to apprehend that turning of the mind to be coupled with a turning of the body, dropping to our knees before the lord, touching our heads to the floor in an act that unifies once again our minds and our bodies—pairing both in submission to Christ's most loving presence—which is both now and ever.

As our father among the saints, Saint Ephrem of Syria has prayed, we also pray:

O Lord and Master of my life, grant not unto me the spirit of idleness,
of discouragement, of lust for power, and of vain-speaking.

Grant, rather, unto me Thy servant the spirit of chastity,
of meekness, of patience, and of love.

Yea, O Lord and King, grant that I may perceive
my own transgressions, and judge not my brother,
for blesséd are you, unto the ages of ages. Amen.

SCRIPTURE

Psalm 81, 82, 119:97–120;
Jeremiah 8:18–9:7;
Romans 5:1–11;
John 8:12–20

AFFLICTION IS A VERY DIFFICULT MATTER FOR us to consider—so much so, that we oftentimes imagine that, if we were to live in a certain, careful, self-concerned way, we might avoid it altogether, elude it, or escape it. Historically and at present, more than a few mistaken teachers of the faith have—intentionally or not—identified Christian life with comfort and pleasure; some have even identified it with affluence.

On the other hand, the psalmist, the prophets, and our beloved saints have observed and have suggested a somewhat more severe teaching. The fathers and the mothers of our church have added to this teaching their own voices—and their lives. We are not called to lives of comfort, even if we nonetheless are called to lives of joy.

It is this deep, bass note of joy that sustains us despite our sufferings and our afflictions. We may find ourselves moving through the darkness, but our paths are, even so, illumined by his light. Such suffering, in fact, becomes a means of apprehending God's grace. "Suffering," writes Saint Paul, "produces perseverance; perseverance, character; and character, hope."

Among the many perplexities of the scriptures, one passage in Saint Paul's epistle to the Colossians proves very perplexing indeed. He writes: "Now I rejoice in my sufferings for your sake, and in my flesh I complete what is lacking in the afflictions of Christ for the sake of his body, which is the Church."

One cannot help but wonder, of course, *what* could possibly be lacking from the afflictions of Christ? What—offering a more likely translation for *isterímata*, the word Saint Paul uses—"is yet to be done"?

It could be that what is *so far* lacking is our own participation in his suffering, our intentional partaking of it. We don't yet know him as we might because we don't yet *feel* his love, have not yet acquired a heart like his, an exceedingly merciful heart.

"What is a merciful heart?" writes Saint Isaak of Syria. "It is a heart on fire for the whole of creation, for humanity, for the birds, for the animals, for demons, and for all that exists. At the recollection and at the sight of them, such a person's eyes overflow with tears owing to the fervor of the compassion that grips his heart; as a result of his deep mercy, his heart aches, and cannot bear to observe any injury or slightest suffering of anything in creation.

"This is why he constantly offers up prayer full of tears, even for the irrational animals and for the enemies of truth, even for those who harm him, praying that they be protected and find mercy. He prays [thus] as a result of the great mercy and compassion that is poured out beyond measure—after the likeness of God—in his heart."

This season of self-assigned affliction—of voluntary privation and poverty—has a quiet way of softening the heart. This is yet another of the blessings of Lenten observance, that we might be brought more readily to tears, that we might find our hearts breaking—like his—for the sake of all.

O Most Merciful, open my eyes to the suffering of
others,
that I, like you, might partake of their pain, and
thereby
observe a glimpse of all that you have done for
me.
O Most Longsuffering, may I apprehend the
affliction of your creation,
that I, like you, may ache for its recovery.
O Most Compassionate, give me tears
with which to soften the hardened soil of my
heart.
For you are the Lover of Humankind,
Father, Son, and Holy Spirit. Amen.

Third Thursday of Lent

SCRIPTURE
Psalm 42, 43, 83, 85, 86;
Jeremiah 10:11–24;
Romans 5:12–21;
John 8:21–32

I N TODAY'S READING FROM SAINT PAUL'S LETTER
to the Romans, we come upon a great and subtle mystery—
having to do with the nowadays ubiquitous occasions of sin and
death. In Adam's sinning, he is said to have died; his choice to

disobey appears to have severed his life-sustaining connection to the God who is the source of life. And even as Adam wandered about in exile thereafter, he was, in every way that matters, dead.

As a result of Adam's having sinned and having died, we also are born dying; we also are, in every way that matters, dead; and we therefore also wander about cut off from life— because of which we have no difficulty sinning on our own. "As sin entered into the world through one man, and death through sin, death passed to everyone, *because of which* all sinned."

That is to say, we do not—according to Saint Paul—inherit Adam's sin, *per se*, nor do we inherit his guilt; we do, however, inherit death, an illness unto death. It is due to this death—this fact that our entire race and all attendant creation have been, by Adam's sin, cut off from life—that we *all* subsequently fall into culpability and further alienation. What's to stop us?

Cut off from life, we die. Being dead, we sin. Cracked at birth, we are obliged to break and shatter, and sometimes seem inclined to rush to our demise.

Do we die because we sin, or do we sin because we have been cut off from life?

Is this point moot?

Maybe not.

What if we could be restored, reattached to life, mystically rejoined to the very source of all that lives? What if our desiccated, dwindling persons could be re-infused with living waters? Might we find that we are thereby less inclined to sin? Might we find within our dim confines a freeing glimpse of light? Might we apprehend how even our due sadness becomes in some way bright?

The fathers and the mothers of our church say yes. The fathers and the mothers of the church demonstrate, by their increasingly efficacious lives, that this is so.

This is, moreover, the teaching of the gospel, without Christ, we will simply "die in [our] sins." If, however, we "remain in [Christ's] word," we will "know the truth, and the truth will set [us] free."

Free from death, yes, but also free from sin. It's possible.

Saint Isaak writes, "Repentance is the mother of life. It opens its door to us when we take flight from all things. The grace that we have lost after baptism, by leading lax lives, repentance renews in us through the discernment of the understanding. By water and spirit we have put on Christ, though we did not perceive his glory. Through repentance we enter into his delight by means of the discerning knowledge that dawns within us."

For many of us, repentance has become something of an afterthought, as if our Christian lives had better things—certainly more pleasant matters—upon which to focus. So long as we neglect this particular grace, we will continue to be subdued by sin and death; however, as soon as we understand that repentance is itself the agent of our recovery from the illness of sin—on that very day—we find joy in virtue, delight in prayer, and we find the light of the Resurrection already illuminating our journey to the cross.

> Holy God, Holy Mighty, Holy Immortal,
>   Have mercy on me.
>
> Help, O God, my unbelief.
> Heal, O Lord, my wounded soul.
> Raise me up from sin and death.

Recover for me, O Lover of Mankind,
exceeding joy in pleasing You, my God.

Holy God, Holy Mighty, Holy Immortal,
Have mercy on me.

Glory to the Father, and to the Son, and to the Holy
Spirit,
both now, and ever, and unto the ages of ages.
Amen.

Third Friday of Lent

SCRIPTURE
Psalm 88, 91, 92 95;
Jeremiah 11:1–8, 14–20;
Romans 6:1–11;
John 8:33–47

THIS, THEN, IS WHAT WE HAVE RECEIVED, WHAT we are at this moment receiving: life and abundant life.

This is how we know it: we have within our reach the power to become dead to sin, to be freed from sin, and from the shame that habitual sin inevitably leaves in its wake. The strongest man or woman in the world is not nearly strong enough to evade sin simply by turning *from* it. In fact, simply turning *from* a thing initiates an already negative disposition.

Actual repentance—a turning that serves—is seldom obtained by simply *turning away*. Instead, we find our strength and our victory in turning *toward*—most specifically in *turning toward* and *leaning into* a very loving, very much present Christ.

He is, of course, ever present and ever near. And everything we think, speak, and do is thought, spoken, and done before him. There is no hidden sin. I have a sense that, when anyone descends into prayer, he or she becomes aware of this, duly convinced. I also have a sense that, when we withdraw from prayer and move back into the flux and chatter of our dissipated lives, we are very likely to be less aware of his nearness—even if that nearness remains both constant and absolute. This failed apprehension of his presence is what allows us to continue in sin, and our continuing sin is what allows us to insufficiently apprehend His presence.

I also suppose that, even then, we have sufficient sense that a choice remains. We sin only when we accede to sin. I know—from my own, not-always-laudable experience—sin happens only when I agree to it.

The fathers make a very useful distinction between our having a passing, sinful thought and our committing a sin. They speak of the matter as if such thoughts are unavoidable—as I find they are—but can be pushed aside through watchfulness and prayer, through our turning deliberately to Christ in prayer.

If, on the other hand, the thought arrives, is allowed to linger, allowed to develop, and become the center of our attention, that is when sin is committed.

And that is when whatever progress we have made in the interim is tossed aside, unceremoniously squandered.

The trick to maintaining our progress into abundant life comes down to our maintaining prayer, and with it an acute sense of Christ's presence.

In his book *The Sacrament of Love*, one of my favorite theologians, Paul Evdokimov writes, "It is not enough to say prayers, one must become, be prayer, prayer incarnate.... A saint is not a superman, but one who discovers and lives his truth as a liturgical being."

Yes, he does work wonders for the dead. He has worked wonders for us. Have we been delivered into new life—as children and not as slaves—only to squander, repeatedly, that vast blessing? Do we make a little progress in the divine ascent only to slip back to the bottom rung?

Probably.

This need not be the case. We have received, and are this moment receiving, life, abundant life. We can take it or leave it.

I vote we take it.

Through prayer, we are allowed to grasp life himself and hold onto him, saying ever and again, "I will not let you go, until you bless me." And he will.

O ever present God, strengthen my will, that I may become
increasingly watchful, alert to all that would impede
my knowing, ever, how near you are.

O most near God, teach me to pray, enable me
to lean into your presence, and to keep
my mind and heart attached to you.

For you are the source of life and health, the hope of all who pass through affliction.

Glory to the Father, and to the Son, and to the Holy Spirit. Amen.

Third Saturday of Lent

SCRIPTURE
Psalm 87, 90, 136;
Jeremiah 13:1–11;
Romans 6:12–23;
John 8:47–59

THIS WEEK FOLLOWING THE SUNDAY OF THE Holy Cross is one in which we continue to examine our own hearts, to recognize and to admit—as fully as we are able— the degree to which our "missings of the mark" have led to our continued squandering of abundant life; it is a time when we are obliged to acknowledge the extent to which we have settled for small things over great, illness over health.

This week, however, proves something of a pivot point as well; it is a time when we seek to realize the connection between this sin of ours—our severance from life, our penchant for death— and Christ's appalling Incarnation and crucifixion.

Death, it turns out, is why he came. Our death is, in fact, what he came to overcome.

His love for us is what occasioned his so doing in appalling condescension.

He is the vine, and we, the severed branches going dry. His Incarnation has grafted our being once more onto the source of life, himself. His crucifixion will accept the death that we are due, the death that we ourselves have both inherited and chosen, the death that keeps us broken within ourselves and separate from every other. In that dire confrontation, death will do its work; death will do what it has always done to these our frail frames.

This time, however, death won't keep, won't take. Death won't prove this time—nor ever after—to be the final word. The uncontainable has entered into death's meager grip, and he has broken it.

He has *undone death by death*, we say.

The Lenten road continues, and we have reached the halfway point. We are probably exhausted, have met the extent of our own, insufficient strength. We are, almost certainly, unable to proceed under our own power. This is, perhaps, the greatest lesson of Lenten observance: that we *need* him—for everything. Even to rise from bed, even to place one foot before the other, and surely to do our daily tasks.

This is hard. This is very hard.

But if we do it—assisted by his presence and by prayer—we will obtain an uncommon sense of how difficult was the way *he* walked. We will feel some measure of the exhaustion that surely must have weighed on *him*. In that affliction, we will find a new, renewing sense of our union with him. And we will find our own weaknesses shored up by his unremitting strength.

To the Romans, Saint Paul writes, "The wages of sin is death, but the free gift of God is eternal life in Christ Jesus our Lord."

To the Pharisees, Christ says, "Whoever keeps my word will never see death."

The psalmist writes, "The Lord loves the gates of Zion, His foundation on the holy mountains.... Indeed, it shall be said of Zion that every man was born there. He, the Most High, will preserve it."

The Lord appears to love his dwelling place, and we appear to be that very place, that sacred place—the city of God, where all our persons meet the One, and live.

His steadfast love is eternal.

> Loving God,
>   Whose mercy exceeds justice,
>   Whose life breaks the bonds of death,
>   Who makes of His people a dwelling place,
> I pray, O Holy One,
>   that I may walk this path with you,
>   that I may taste and see,
>   that I may partake of life himself,
>   and pass with him through death.
> Glory to the Father, and to the Son, and to the Holy Spirit,
>   both now, and ever, and unto the ages of ages.
> Amen.

FOURTH WEEK OF
LENT

Beth Bevis

History of the Feast

Fourth Sunday of Lent / Laetare Sunday

T HE FOURTH SUNDAY OF LENT, KNOWN AS Laetare Sunday in the Western church, offers a foretaste of Easter joy and a reminder that fasting during Lent is about nurturing the spiritual life, not about self-denial for its own sake. By now we have reached the midway point of the Lenten season— Laetare Sunday is also known as "Mid-Lent Sunday"—and we are likely to feel some weariness from the sustained processes of self-examination, fasting, and prayer. But the opening words of the liturgy on this Sunday, "Laetare Jerusalem" (Rejoice, O Jerusalem), invite us to find joy in the midst of trial.

In some churches, the altar is decorated with flowers on Laetare Sunday, and clergy are permitted to wear rose-colored vestments instead of the usual purple that represents the solemnity of the Lenten season. These traditions visually represent the joy for which the somber character of the rest of Lent prepares us. Falling midway through the forty days, Laetare Sunday is a reminder that our practices of penance and fasting are oriented toward joy, toward the ultimate celebration of resurrection and redemption at Easter, and that the aim of our fasting is not spiritual fatigue but rejuvenation.

Mid-Lent Sunday is known by other names, each of which brings associated traditions that highlight this day's tone of joyful anticipation and refreshment. In England, this day is known as

Mothering Sunday, a name that probably originated from the tradition among members of far-flung parishes to return to the Cathedral, or "mother church," on the middle Sunday of Lent. Mothering Sunday has since become a day to honor mothers, and today grown children in England still mark the day by returning home to visit their mothers, bringing flowers and small gifts, and celebrating with a family meal.

Laetare Sunday has also been known as Refreshment Sunday because of the various forms of refreshment represented by this day's traditions—from the relaxation of fasting obligations to the consumption of special treats. One traditional treat in England and France is the simnel cake, a pastry made of fine flour and dried fruits and frosted with marzipan or almond paste. These cakes have been baked during Lent and Easter since medieval times.

Concrete gestures of nourishment and refreshment unite these various ways of signaling the middle of Lent. Indeed, Laetare Sunday's associations with both mothering and refreshment are rooted in the traditional readings of today's liturgy. In Paul's letter to the Galatians, we read of Jerusalem as "the mother of us all." And until the adoption of the common lectionary the gospel reading used in the Catholic tradition for this day was the story of the feeding of the five thousand. In this way, Laetare Sunday reminds us that the Christian tradition of fasting and self-denial during Lent is always supplemented by God's nourishment, strengthening us in our spiritual and physical efforts. Designated for celebration and refreshment, this day not only offers a reprieve from the rigors of Lenten fasting; it reminds us that the purpose of the fast is to prepare us to receive and more fully enjoy God's blessings.

Fourth Sunday of Lent

SCRIPTURE
Psalm 19, 46, 66, 67;
Jeremiah 14:1–9, 17–22;
Galatians 4:21–5:1;
Mark 8:11–21

THERE ARE NORWAY PINES ON THE YARD JUST outside my window. One is quite thoroughly dead, and the other three aren't in good shape. I'm not sure what's attacking them, but it seems that, sooner or later, the owner of this place we're renting is going to have to take them all down, which is sad because trees are much beloved in the tall-grass prairie country where we live, a place where, once upon a time, the grass was a seemingly endless ocean. Trees themselves are rare; a stand of graceful Norway pines are almost an angel's visitation.

Weeds grow up like awkward rubber necks beneath the branches of those pines. I can hardly get at them because the thorny lower branches come armed with barbed wire. This morning, at least some of the dead branches extending from the house side of the tree are history; I cut them down yesterday. The best you could say for them was they created some interesting lines, but that wasn't enough. This morning, they're firewood.

If you were, with me, to look out my patio door most any hour of the day, if you were to see those Norway pines, the out-of-control, scrawny-as-skeleton weeds beneath them, and the gray-green grass all around, you'd have to admit, with me, that there is nothing particularly comely about the still life just outside—lots of death and decay actually, and a few weeds that, left unchecked, will only grow more boisterous.

Yet, come dawn, what I see outside this window is, most mornings, almost regal, because, as anyone with a camera knows, once the buttery morning sun graces anything, the whole world is worth a look.

Photography, saith this total amateur, is really all about light— managing it, in a way, even though natural light can't be managed.

Five minutes from now those same Norway pines, dressed gaudily by the dawn into something even Photoshop can't mimic, will have stripped off their golden wardrobe, only to be clothed in different apparel altogether. So, really, what tickles my fancy about this otherwise mundane peek at a depressing, dying world, is made ticklish by the tender grace of yellowy-soft heavenly light.

When the morning sun burnishes even these dying Norway pines, it dresses them out in the finest apparel they'll ever don, a golden splash of dawn this early morning—and a reminder, even for a moment, of heavenly joy.

The fourth Sunday of Lent, known as Laetare Sunday in the Western church, offers a foretaste of Easter joy, like dawn's early light in my own backyard, a reminder that fasting during Lent is about nurturing a view that sees the world God has given us bedecked in his own blessed artistry.

Jeremiah's tortured lament in chapter 14 ends not simply in a petition for joy, but a testimony to the very light of the world: "Therefore our hope is in you, for you are the one who does all this."

It's mid-Lent Sunday, and we're capable of feeling the blues. But this Sabbath morning we're invited to turn out heads just a bit and see the joy amid our trials, to celebrate what is surely to come—

rebirth at Easter. The golden morning sun on the Norway pines just outside my door is a blessing sure as life, new life, and Easter.

> Each and every glimpse we witness of your love, Lord, is only a fleeting fragment of your eternal radiance. Still, for those moments—for the brightness of dawn in the darkness of our lives, for music that makes our spirits dance, for the hallowed touch of those we love—we thank you, loving Father, because we know that all the goodness itself has its origin in you. In this Lenten season, help us turn away from ourselves to see ever more clearly the outlines of your face in every moment of our lives. Forgive our foolish pride. Send us your grace so that we may see the dawn in our lives this Easter season.

Fourth Monday of Lent

SCRIPTURE
*Psalm 89;
Jeremiah 16:10–21;
Romans 7:1–12;
John 6:1–15*

WE WERE STANDING IN AN OLD COUNTRY church in South Dakota—stamped tin ceilings and ancient oak pews. Once upon a time two wings had been added on either side for extra seating. The carpet was new, the paint fresh, but the place was old for white-settler South Dakota, 130 years. No matter how diligently the people kept it up, this house of worship showed its age.

My immigrant great-grandparents once walked weekly through the same front doors, then sat, five kids with them, beneath the same tin ceilings. I have a history in this old church; that's what I was thinking. I may well have been the first great-grandchild ever to darken the front door, but some particle of me was once here some generations ago.

We'd just come from a long day along the Missouri River— some hiking, some sight-seeing on the valley's big and gorgeous shoulders—before stopping at a woebegone country church in a town well down the road toward dying. It was early June, the sun radiant, the emerald land we'd been driving through quite empty of distraction and therefore, honestly, full of God.

An old psalm hymn bubbled up in my soul from somewhere in my childhood. I never considered it a favorite, hadn't thought about it for years or sung it for decades. Long ago it was chased from the hymnal by more peppy stuff, but somehow it seemed apt for time and circumstance.

So I asked our guests whether they remembered "To the Hills I Lift My Eyes" from an old psalter. Most of our fellow travelers were around long enough to remember, although faintly, the melody I was offering. They nodded politely, enough of an assent; besides I was not to be denied. I grabbed a pitch out of nowhere, and soon they were all singing with me because the first few lines hadn't left anyone's memory and the melody is simple. We pieced together the lyrics because some of us knew enough that all of us found a path through.

The bright sun outside created midsummer heat and not a whisper of night, but I remembered Asaph's voice in Psalm 77—"I remembered my songs in the night." Even today, that line reminds me of that moment in that old church, and the blessedness of connecting with something greater than me or us or any of our individual stories, something ethereal that perhaps can be carried only in music. Beatitude in such unreasonable things is sometimes the richest of gifts.

One of the comforts of faith begins in our fulsome sense of our belonging; we are not alone because we know whose we are. "So, my brothers," Paul says, heavy on the *brothers*, "you also died to the law through the body of Christ." And why? "So that you might belong to another, to him who was raised from the dead." But there's more: "that we might bear fruit to God."

Sometimes that fruit emerges most fully in music, even in an old dying church in the middle of nowhere, a place set gloriously in God's world, the God to whom we belong.

All that beauty reminded me as it does us, brothers and sisters, now through Lent, that once—and always—there was and is joy.

Refresh us with your holiness, Lord. Give us the vision to acknowledge anew that beneath every inch of what we see and every word of what we know, a broad and loving hand is ever there to hold us in the divine entirety of your endless love, and that, gloriously, we are your children and you are the God to whom we belong. Amen.

SCRIPTURE
Psalm 91, 94, 99;
Jeremiah 17, 19–27;
Romans 7:13–25;
John 6:16–27

BEFORE THE BATTLE THAT WOULD FOREVER change Native American life on the Great Plains, the Battle at Greasy Grass—or Little Big Horn—Sitting Bull, a Lakota medicine man, cut chunks of his own flesh from his arms and legs as an act of devotion to the divine, *Wakan Tanka.*

Bloodied and weakened, he then saw a vision of cavalrymen falling from the sky. That vision, historians say, strengthened Lakota resolve for the battle to come.

To most, what he did seems barbaric and heathenish, yet it's understandable to the soul. What Sitting Bull did that day was surrender, sacrifice bloodily, humbling himself in deep contrition and submission to the divine.

Mother Teresa was little more than a child when she scribbled these lines while aboard a ship on her very first trip to India.

Fine and pure as summer dew
Her soft warm tears begin to flow,
Sealing and sanctifying now
Her painful sacrifice.

She had to be immensely anxious about the world she was entering and what was to come. She was little older than college freshmen, away from home for the first time; and I've seen them cry in torrents.

What's difficult for me to understand, however, is "her painful sacrifice." If she deeply valued what she might have become had she *not* chosen to take her orders, being on her way to a new life in India would have seemed more difficult. She was soon to become, after all, "the little bride of Christ," something she desired passionately.

Yet her tears, "pure as the summer dew," flowed from what she calls her "painful sacrifice."

I don't think Mother Teresa ever pulled out some kind of poetic license or wrenched out half-truths or hyperbole, and I can certainly see her there on the ship's deck, little more than a kid, a hanky dabbing at her eyes.

With so much of her storied life yet in front of her, chapters of weighty aching yet to come, and love in volumes still to be given away, it's still difficult for me to understand exactly what she meant. What I don't understand is her *sacrifice*.

But then, I just returned from the gym, where I work out lest my weight balloon. Our house is comfy and warm. Sometime this week, I'm getting a new La-Z-Boy. Tuesdays and Wednesdays are tough teaching days for me, but I'll come out whole by the weekend. I haven't cut out chunks of flesh as of late, haven't denied myself anything to speak of, and haven't fasted all that assiduously. Frankly, I doubt I know much at all about suffering.

But somewhere lately, we sang the old hymn "I Surrender All." "Really?" I asked myself. "I do?"

How much of me, exactly, is in Jeremiah's surrender: "Heal

me, Lord, and I will be healed; save me and I will be saved, for
you are the one I praise."

Maybe I don't recognize Mother Teresa's sacrifice because I
haven't a clue about my own.

Maybe.

> Lord of heaven and earth, king of mountain peaks
> and ocean's depths, sovereign of all time and
> space, accept this confession of my insignificance
> as the devotion of a humbled sinner who has lost a
> definition of sacrifice. Keep me on my knees, Lord,
> in heartfelt praise. Amen.

Fourth Wednesday of Lent

SCRIPTURE
Psalm 101, 109:1–4, 20–30, 119:121–144;
Jeremiah 18:1–11;
Romans 8:1–11;
John 6:27–40

I WISH I HAD A BETTER HANDLE ON *RIGHTEOUSNESS*,
a word which has largely gone out of usage, even though its
contrary, self-righteousness, seems to prosper. Much of today's
reading is about righteousness—how good it is, how different,
how comforting: "The mind of sinful man is death, but the mind
controlled by the Spirit is life and peace," so says Paul to the Romans.

I only wish righteousness was always clearly perceptible, not just in others, but in me, too.

Only once in my life have I walked through the valley of the shadow of death, and that was a few years ago, when I sat for several days at the bedside of my father who was dying. I knew those days were his last, even though the doctors and nurses wouldn't say it exactly and my family couldn't believe it—after all, what had brought him to the hospital was only searing back pain.

But I knew he wasn't going to step out of that bed again because he became less and less communicative, less and less there. We never had a final talk. We never spoke in that blissful way most of us fantasize might happen in the final moments we share with those we love.

I helped him when he needed to drink, when he needed to urinate, when he felt deep pain, but I don't think he knew I was there. The intensity of his pain and the effort his body was mounting simply to stay alive drew all of his strength and conscious will.

Only those who've been there will understand what I mean when I say that those days were among the best of my life. Maybe things weren't said that could or should have been, and, sure, if I could rewrite the scene, I would. But I don't remember another time in our lives together when I simply sat beside him, the man who had given me life and always loved me, even when I didn't deserve it.

A man came in one afternoon, a man from my father's church. I knew him from my childhood, but he wouldn't have been the man I thought the church might send. He was my father's district elder, and it was his job, I know, to visit him.

But he was there. I told him my father likely wouldn't know he was there.

But that didn't stop him. This burly guy I remember as a truck driver walked up to the bedside, took my father's hand, and spoke to him as if my father understood every last word, even tried to engage him in conversation that didn't have a chance of starting. And when he realized that, this burly angel of mercy simply kept talking himself, told my father that throughout his own life he'd always looked up to Dad, told him how he'd been one of those men he'd call truly godly, how much he'd meant to him, a model of a Christian love.

A big man with his hair square as a GI, a guy I had some trouble thinking of as an elder, a man I don't know that I'd ever spoken to before—that man looked into my father's agonized face, held my father's hand, and told him in no uncertain terms that as far as he was concerned, my father had modeled Jesus Christ in Oostburg, Wisconsin, which is to say, righteousness.

And then he backed away, looked at me, shook my hand, and left, wiping tears from his eyes.

I don't know whether any of that got into my father's mind, or whether he heard those words or picked up the warmth of the big hand that held his. My guess is he didn't, but I don't know. The nurses told me they'd often been surprised by what people in my father's condition did hear.

But I heard it—every single word of that truck driver's testimony—and I am reminded of it when I think about that line about how the Lord will walk with me through the valley of the shadow of death.

What I know is that that day, he sent my father and me a righteous man who happened to be a truck driver.

In this Lenten season, Lord, draw our attention to you and your way. Keep us off the paths that lead us away from you, no matter what lies at their ends. Bring us home to the reality of your death and, incredibly, your resurrection. Cleanse us. Fill us with your righteousness that we may be holy. Amen.

Fourth Thursday of Lent

SCRIPTURE
Psalm 69:1–23, 31–38;
Psalm 73;
Jeremiah 22:13–23;
Romans 8:12–27;
John 6:41–51

FOR THREE DAYS, THE CHILD BLED PROFUSELY from the nose. She was six years old, and doctors had no idea what was causing the bleeding. What's more, they understood that if the bleeding didn't stop, her life was in grave danger.

The year was 1913. The doctors knew little about transfusion, but they understood the importance of somehow getting good new blood back into the little girl's system, so they asked her father, a preacher, to give his daughter some of his. He did, one of the first blood transfusions in the state of Michigan.

The yellowed newspaper story is titled "Minister Saves the Life of Daughter By Giving Blood," and it ends by explaining how the father "was considerably improved and was able to dress." Then it adds, "The child was also considerably better and hopes are entertained for her recovery."

Two weeks later she was dead. Little Agnes Gertrude, my grandparents' oldest child, succumbed once the hemorrhaging returned. For a time her father's blood had brightened her face and her possibilities, but his gift—as unusual and strange to the newspaper readers as it must have been to him—wasn't enough to save her life.

Family lore says the doctors knew very little, back then, about blood-typing. Her father, my relatives speculate, was as good a choice as the doctors could have made, but what coursed in his veins was not a match. Agnes Gertrude, my aunt, died two weeks after that strange new procedure the doctors called "a transfusion."

I have no newspaper accounts of my grandparents' grief, but I know some oral history. Agnes's sister told me how her father, a man of God, lay face down on the rug of the living room for almost a week after Agnes's death, unable to move. Who could blame him—for an entire afternoon, he lay there beside his little girl, his blood flowing into her veins. My aunt remembered his profound grief, told me he was lethargic, depressed, his whole countenance darkened by the death of his child.

Nothing changed, she said, until he accepted a call to another congregation, a small country church up north. She told me how she remembered riding in a horse-drawn wagon up to that country church, their possessions packed up behind them, and there being greeted by the entire congregation there on the lawn, all of them waiting for the new preacher and his family.

"And that was it," she told me. The darkness ended.

I can't imagine it was completely over. If my grandparents were still alive, I'd love to be able to question them about their loss, if they could talk about it even a century later. But what my aunt told me I've never forgotten; the darkness ended on a summer day on the lawn of a country church full of welcoming people.

There is immense lament in the readings for today, so much so that the sheer weight of it feels as if the sadness of the world sits squarely on our shoulders. And somehow our lament is made even worse by comparisons we seemingly can't help making: amid our tangled woes, others all around appear to prosper.

Things get that way for some of us, for most of us, even for all of us at one time or another—so much suffering, so much injustice, so much loss.

There's so much grief, the heart gives out. "My flesh and my heart may fail," the psalmist says, but then comes the relief, "but God is the strength of my heart and my portion forever."

Be our refuge, Lord. Keep us near. Bring us home to a lawn full of smiling people who open their loving arms.

This is your world, Lord. Bless us with that assurance even when the grief or sadness darkens our vision. Be our refuge. Keep us near. We are not alone, Lord. We are never alone when you hold us in your hand. Amen.

SCRIPTURE

Psalm 95, 102, 107:1–32;
Jeremiah 23:1–8;
Romans 8:28–39;
John 6:52–59

THERE WERE MOMENTS YESTERDAY WHEN I FELT a notion of what a real Lakota giveaway might have been like 150 years ago, moments when I wanted simply to forget the $1 price tag on this or that piece of jetsam we were peddling at our first-ever garage sale.

Long before any white people lived here, this was Lakota land, where giveaways happened ritually, at the deaths of family members, for instance. Garage sales happen ritually here too, every last weekend in April, but they're not prompted by death or joy or some taste of a brand new life—and very little is *given* away.

We are neither reenactors nor wannabes. My wife was not wearing a blanket nor I a loincloth, thank goodness. Almost everything we sold we won't miss. We were lightening the burden.

A real Lakota giveaway, the kind that may have been practiced right here, was no garage sale. Sometimes they'd even give away horses, the most precious commodity Native Siouxlanders owned.

I first read about the Lakota giveaway on a Sunday morning, in a big book about the Yankton Sioux. Giveaways were a means by which people gained stature. Those men and women rich enough in spirit to simply give away what they valued grew in esteem because of their devout care for the poor, an ethic practiced right here before my great-grandparents lugged the New Testament along into the hinterland and talked about what Jesus said about those less blessed than we are.

By 1870, when my great-grandparents came, white folks had determined giveaways to be illegal, a heathen ritual from which those savages had to be saved. That Sunday morning I first read about them, we marched off to church for what was, I remember, a wonderful sermon about our materialism, the kind of sermon a century ago we might have seen in practice had we not determined the Yankton should give up their heathen ways.

That's what I thought about, out back, at our moving sale yesterday, how just for a moment I had a sense—a fleeting sense—of a real giveaway, the kind of thing that would have happened here long, long ago.

We didn't make bundles of money, and I never shed a tear for anything people carted off. Now my brand new Dell laptop—that would be another story. Or the samurai sword my father took home from the South Pacific at the end of World War II, or the ancient Navajo rug my grandfather got in New Mexico, or our bank account, our stocks and bonds, our IRAs? Had those things been out there on the driveway to be taken for the asking, then it would have been a giveaway in the tradition of the Yankton Sioux.

We didn't do that. You think we're crazy?

Anyway, standing outside yesterday, a perfect April afternoon, I couldn't help think of the tall grass prairie just as full of people, Native people, coming by and looking around, all of them smiling.

Real worth belongs to the creator, or so says the psalmist—"you laid the foundations of the earth and the heavens are the work of your hands."

You can't read that line without punching out the pronouns. Because even those foundations will perish, he says; "they will be discarded."

Our first-ever yard sale, yesterday, was really a kind of Lenten exercise, to stand there amid the flotsam and jetsam out on the lawn and to see myself in those perishables, so deeply committed to the stuff that clutters my life, to recognize the disposable gods I worship.

> We will never know abundance without your love, Lord, because we will never prosper until we know the dire poverty of life without you. Glory and honor, praise and adoration—now and forever more be yours. Amen.

Fourth Saturday of Lent

SCRIPTURE
Psalm 107:33–43; 108:1–6;
Jeremiah 23:9–15;
Romans 9:1–8;
John 6:60–71

ON HIS WAY HOME FROM HIS JOB AT THE packing plant, Phet had to cross the Missouri River, then travel up the freeway toward his home in Morningside. Along the way, stood—well, floated—a huge and comely riverboat casino, the finest, fanciest gambling joint in the region. Sometimes—often, by his recounting—he'd stop and spend the rest of the day and night amid the smoky jangling slots. He wasn't stressing his marriage; often as not, his wife was right there at his side.

Then he became a Christian, left the casino, lost his wife, and gained another. When I asked him what it meant to be a Christian, he answered by drawing out the dimensions of his new life. Although he was still working at the packing plant, he was living in a new house with a new wife, and he was going to church, had become a deacon. But mostly, to Phet, being a Christian meant he no longer stopped at the riverboat. He was done with all that, done with gambling.

Deacon Phet got himself enabled.

Sasumu Nashimoto, a petty thief from Yokohama, Japan, used to listen to Christian radio while doing all kinds of late-night petty theft. One night he was going after some stuff behind a factory when he started to think about the clear plastic that stretched over waste materials, the stuff he grabbed and sold elsewhere, putting the bucks in his own pockets. If that plastic were black, not clear, he thought, he could really turn a profit. But who could create a miracle like that, he thought, chuckling.

With his truck radio playing a sermon, he kept mulling over the question, who turns black to white? Who can create miracles? Why, only God can. It came to him as a revelation, he told me. Today, no longer a criminal, he's a leader in his faith community.

Elder Nashimoto got himself enabled, too.

The novelist Walker Percy's genealogy of distinguished ancestors still overflows with grim sadness—Civil War heroes, Mississippi statesmen, and two unforgettable suicides. Both his father and his grandfather ended their lives with a shotgun. Two years after his father's death, Percy's mother was killed in an automobile accident.

For a profession, Walker Percy, a medical doctor, chose to be a pathologist, someone whose daily work meant working over corpses. But early on in his profession, he contracted tuberculosis, spent some years at a sanitarium, read Kierkegaard and Dostoyevsky, among others, then converted to Christianity in 1947.

Walker Percy was enabled also.

I don't know everything there is to know about Walker Percy, but I believe I can guess, given the outline of his life and the themes of his novels, how Percy too might think about this line from today's readings because he must have felt himself, in his own way, enabled: "No one can come to me unless the Father has enabled them."

A cloud of witnesses all around profess their faith through a spacious library of stories, none of them exactly the same except in divine trajectory. What astonishes me is the sheer breadth of the experience of the Christian faith; there's a million stories because the faith itself is immensely spacious, even though all of those stories end in redemption.

There is so much elbow room in how it is we come to faith, space enough for all our stories. Nobody's stripes are exactly the same, but somehow we all get healed; we all are enabled.

We all read the same intent in Christ's words in John 6, but we piece together that meaning with an unending list of experiences, each of which recount just exactly how it was that we too found ourselves so divinely enabled.

There is no end to your grace, Lord. You handle each of us with kid gloves. With your love, you enable us to come to you. Only in your light can we see down the road. For your gifts of vision and direction, we promise our devotion and service. In Christ alone, amen.

FIFTH WEEK OF
LENT

**Fifth Sunday
of Lent/Saint
Mary of Egypt**

(formerly Passion Sunday)

I N THE EASTERN ORTHODOX TRADITION, THE FIFTH
Sunday of Lent is observed as a holy day honoring Saint
Mary of Egypt (AD 344–421). For Orthodox Christians as well
as for Catholics and Anglicans, Saint Mary is the patron saint of
penitents. Leaving behind a life of prostitution, she spent forty-
seven years wandering the desert in Egypt after her conversion.
During Lent a year before her death, she encountered a priest
in the desert and asked him to return the following year so that
she could receive Communion. The priest returned on Holy
Thursday, and just before dying, Mary received the sacrament for
which she had waited.

The placement of Mary's saint day near the end of Lent
provides an opportunity to reflect on the parallels between
Lent and the life of the saints. In Mary, we find an example
of a penitent on a journey that ended in satisfaction. If we
are weary from our own acts of penance, we can remember
Saint Mary's strength and be encouraged that what awaits us
at the end of our journey is, as it was for her, forgiveness and
fulfillment.

In the United Kingdom, the fifth Sunday of Lent is known as
Carling Sunday, after the dried peas (carlings) traditionally served
on this day. This Lenten meal may have evolved from an old

English church custom of distributing beans to the community on the fifth Sunday of Lent, then known as Passion Sunday, due to the scarcity of food at midwinter. In any case, eating peas cooked in butter is still a beloved Lenten tradition, especially in Scotland and the north of England. It is yet another reminder of the balanced nature of the fast, a source of nourishment in the midst of Lent.

Until 1969, the fifth Sunday of Lent was known in the Western church as Passion Sunday. This day marked the beginning of Passiontide, the two weeks leading up to Easter. From the Latin word "passio," passion refers to suffering as well as love. On Passion Sunday and the weeks that followed, the church turned its attention to the love that inspired Christ to suffer on behalf of humankind. During Passiontide, statues, crosses, and other religious images were veiled either in red (the color of martyrdom and the Passion) or purple (the color of penitence). In addition, the "Gloria Patri," a short prayer giving glory to God, was omitted from its usual place in daily prayer as a way of acknowledging that Christ traded his glory for humility and suffering.

When the Roman Catholic liturgical calendar shifted the observance of Passion Sunday to the following week, Passion Sunday became simply another name for Palm Sunday. Nevertheless, Christians today might still perceive a shift on this fifth Sunday, which ushers us into the last week of Lent before Holy Week. Throughout Lent, we have been encouraged to reflect on our own shortcomings, turn from our sins, and ready ourselves for Easter with acts of fasting and penance. Now, as we draw nearer to Holy Week, we begin to anticipate with greater urgency the coming events of Christ's death and Resurrection.

Fifth Sunday of Lent

SCRIPTURE

Psalm 118, 145;
Jeremiah 23:16–32;
1 Corinthians 9:19–27;
Mark 8:31–9:1

BY THE FIFTH WEEK OF LENT WE MAY BE EXCUSED for feeling a certain weariness on the journey, but the drama of the season is reaching new highs—and lows. This is a time not simply to praise God for the grace that comes our way, but to explore what happens when life goes awry, and we find ourselves anxious, deprived, even despairing.

But first the highs: Psalm 145, attributed to David, is a full-throated anthem of gratitude. I can hear a choir at work behind the black words on my Bible's white page. The psalmist, like a composer, is finding new forms for his music. The theme? A catalog of God's deeds of power and generosity. The angels are called to praise God. The sun, moon, stars, and even rain are challenged to demonstrate his magnanimity.

And then the tone shifts to those who have been ground down to extremes of poverty and destitution. The psalmist acknowledges that it is the Almighty who upholds those who are falling. He listens and hears their desperate cries. He saves them.

In our church, as in many across the country, we deal with personal disasters at close range—street people who survive barely, living under bridges. But not beyond divine mercy; the prophet Jeremiah describes a God who is both far away and so near by that no one can be out his reach. Even in the nooks and crannies of deprivation and cold he is with them.

On our street corners transients cluster, looking for work. I've met destitute mothers who have been evicted from their apartments and are forced to live in their cars with their kids and sometimes a dog. This is especially hard in winter, and gas is costly. Tearful victims of domestic abuse are on the run, in hiding. Addicts desperate for their drug, as well as those who have chosen the long, hard journey to recovery.

The local food banks and clinics never seem adequate to the need. Our church offers a little financial help—a gas voucher, a bus token—but just as importantly, we engage in counsel and fervent prayer with those who line up once a week in our lobby. We look each one in the eye and listen to each story. We hug them. We hold them close as they weep.

We are only human, but the God of plenitude is listening through us, and we are called to be God's hands and feet and voices, standing in the gap between human need and divine help.

In Mark's Gospel, when Jesus looks ahead and speaks openly about his coming human suffering and rejection, it is more than Peter can stand. Peter considers Jesus's talk about future affliction and rejection as undignified and degrading for one who has identified himself as God's son, God's ambassador.

I can't imagine rebuking Jesus, but that's what loudmouth Peter did, until he got a resounding comeuppance. Such thinking, Jesus told him, calling him a "satan," or antagonist, is pedestrian and faithless, not taking the divine plan into account.

Finally, Paul, writing to his friends in Corinth, voices his own credo: that his commission as Jesus's representative is to be like Jesus—a slave, a Jew, weak, a sufferer—identifying with the lowest of the low in order to welcome them into God's free, strong band of survivors and overcomers.

Loving Jesus, it goes against our human grain to acknowledge weakness and failure. We want so badly to succeed and to be known to succeed. What other people think of us sometimes quells within us the power of your call and commission, to be like you as Christians, to suffer as you did, to acknowledge our inadequacy in the face of enormous challenges. Day by day remind us of your path to Jerusalem to face ultimate suffering and death. Transform our thinking. May your willingness to be defenseless in the face of evil give us courage to face the predicaments of being human, identifying with the strugglers like those you loved and saved. Amen.

SCRIPTURE
Psalm 31, 35;
Jeremiah 24:1–10;
Romans 9:19–33;
John 9:1–17

W HAT STANDS OUT FOR ME IN THESE VARIED verses is the way the spirit of God puts dramatic imagery into the mouths of his spokespersons, who in today's readings are a psalmist, a prophet, a preacher, and an apostle.

God using pictures to build a case is like putting flesh on a skeleton. He turns a principle into a picture. And of course, this happens all through the Bible. It is the Holy Spirit's preferred teaching tool.

How energizing it is that the Bible is pierced through and through with metaphor, analogy, parable, simile, comparison. God is saying, "This is how I bring *my* truth into *your* human reality. My principles, my ways of doing things are clothed in story." Just think how doctrine and dogma ("that which is given") are made more vivid in the context of a narrative; when you hear a homily, a lecture, an address, notice how your ears prick up when the speaker begins to tell a story!

When I first scanned through these verses, some of the words that caught my attention stood out like signal flares: the psalmist thinks of the trustworthiness of God as a rock and a fort, and the tricks of his enemies are snares or traps. But his feet are "steadied" and kept from stumbling when God plants them in

"a broad place." When the psalm writer feels overwhelmed by
the scorn and meanness of others, he feels "like a broken pot" or
"a besieged city." He likens his enemies to hungry lions. Can we
relate to images like those?

Jeremiah, a prophet who learned the hard way all about
betrayal, calls upon the Lord to be "a storm of anger and a
whirling tempest of retribution" on those who refused to listen.
In order to make the divine message clear, God gives the prophet
a *picture* of a basket of figs so rotten they're repulsive, inedible.
All they're good for is to be thrown out on the garbage heap of
God's disgust.

Paul, writing to the Romans, gives us one of the Bible's most
compelling images: God as potter and us as lumps of his clay,
thrown onto his wheel for shaping into artifacts both beautiful
and useful.

Leave it to John to give us the most striking metaphor of
grace—the miracle of sight renewed.

THE SIGHTING
JOHN 9

Out of the shame of spittle,
the scratch of dirt,
he made an anointing.

Oh, it was an agony—the gravel
in the eye, the rude slime, the brittle
clay caked on the soft eyelid.

But with the hurt
light came leaping; in the shock & shine
abstracts took flesh & flew;

winged words like view & space,
shape & shade & green & sky,
bird & horizon & sun

turned real in a man's eye.
Thus was truth given a face
& dark dispelled, & healing done.

Heavenly Father, you who created us to love stories, thank you for all the vividly compelling ways you reveal yourself to us, your children. Thank you for being the Word in the stories. Because we are hard of hearing, you speak shapes and colors into our ears. Like the blind man, we want to see, but when we are myopic, you unlock our vision with your healing salve. Because we are inattentive you direct our attention to something that we cannot ignore, for which we bless your name. Amen.

SCRIPTURE
Psalms 120–127;
Jeremiah 25:8–17;
Romans 10:1–13;
John 9:18–41

DOES IT EVER SEEM TO YOU THAT THE TIRED world of humanity drags on sadly, repeating its successes and its failures like the ticking of an old clock?

Sometimes Lent feels like that to me—a dark time when hopes flicker uncertainly, when all I can feel is my own inadequacy. I want to think of Jesus and the life he lived for me. But though sparks of light and life glimmer occasionally, they are soon extinguished. Do you ever wonder if God is fed up with our pessimism?

I get that impression from today's Jeremiah reading in which God uses imprecatory language to his wayward children. He's saying, "Curse you all for your rebellious spirits. I give up on you. I'm sending you like felons into a prison far from your homeland. See, take this bitter potion, a glass of tainted alcohol that will make you all 'stagger and go out of your minds.'"

With this prophecy began the Jewish people's seventy-year captivity under harsh Babylonian repression.

Imagine the awesome responsibility of proclaiming such a message.

Though its intention is positive—a disciplinary action for their own good with Jeremiah standing in the breach between

God and his erring people—its confrontational nature feels extreme.

It might have been very different. In today's series of triumphant psalms we see a responsive parent who takes action on behalf of his kids when they yell "Help!"

Yes. But to get help you have to admit you're stuck, powerless.

In the Gospel story of the man born blind, though, there's a kind of deliberate irrationality in the onlookers. The man himself not only has his sight back, his whole life has been radically changed from one of painful groping to one of profound relief and gratitude.

Having 20/20 vision translates to this man's greater personal autonomy; now he can *choose* whom to follow. Listen to his word of faith to the skeptics, "This is astonishing! Even though I can suddenly see, you people are still blind to the evidence. Even though it's right in front of you, you can't admit what's happened."

There often remains a vast gap between us in our human blindness and God's willingness to grant clear vision. Yet Paul, in Romans 10, testifies to the utter simplicity of a cry of faith. It's like being let out of prison after long incarceration. Or limping along a dark and dangerous street and being welcomed through an open door into a place of warmth and safety.

Sometimes, in the middle of a writing project, I seem to lose traction, stuck in a blind alley of my own making. My thinking feels pedestrian; I am unmoved by my own argument. Until I shout, "Help!" and open my mind heavenward, I never know what will happen.

OBEDIENCE
When my fingers
know better than I
as they hover over the keyboard,
then type a word that is not
the word I wanted but
a better word—what is that
but an answer. You
caring for details, filling
cracks, your language
arc-ing its swift current
through my bones.

In the deepest part of our hearts, Lord, we know we are not brave or sturdy enough to be in combat with evil and betrayal. Our vision is limited. Only you see and know it all completely. We need your wisdom to tread both the rocky paths and the wild prairies of our lives. Even when we feel safest we may be tripped up by temptation or myopia. Surround us today with your divine protection. Be our scout, our forest ranger. In your powerful name, amen.

SCRIPTURE
Psalm 119:145–176, 128, 129, 130;
Jeremiah 25:30–38;
Romans 10:14–21;
John 10:1–18

I F WE READ TODAY'S SCRIPTURE PASSAGES AS A series of landscapes, what do they seem to have in common? My own mind conjures up, like a series of colored photographs, rolling grassy pastures patched like quilts by stone fences, with the occasional barred gate. And passing through those openings, staff in hand, I see a shepherd with his flock of white, woolly sheep.

I've traveled by car throughout England, Scotland, Ireland, and Wales. I've loved snaking along those narrow lanes between high hedges, and then coming to a fence through which the sheep are close enough to be seen and heard as they energetically crop the green grass. In spring, there are always lambs. Frolicking is the exactly right word to describe them as they leap about, nuzzling at their mothers' teats, innocently playing, unaware of danger.

I've also watched sheep being driven willy-nilly along a dirt road in the Australian outback, blocking the lines of motorists waiting for them to pass. Everywhere, sheep are a funny lot, traditionally viewed as silly, which really means simple, not endowed with substantial brain power, tending to follow each other mindlessly, not knowing better, getting lost. Remember the Jesus story and the song, "There were ninety and nine / that safely lay.... But one was out / in the hills away..."?

My late brother-in-law William was a sheep farmer in New Zealand, and I've watched his crowded flock being herded helplessly into a pen and swiftly sheared, one by one, their fleeces tossed onto piles to be sorted and cleaned and combed and spun into yarn. There's no way the sheep can avoid this shearing. It's fast and forceful. They emerge looking naked, sometimes with bloody streaks from the shears.

During Lent this image reminds me of Jesus, "dumb, like a sheep before the shearers," a lamb without a flaw, a fulfillment of the Old Testament symbolism of a sacrificial animal in the bloody ritual of atonement.

For their flesh and their fleece these animals are valued around the world and throughout history. Sheep also crowd the pages of scripture. The psalmist confesses his own failure: "I have gone astray like a lost sheep." Jeremiah excoriates the false shepherds of God's people, they who have failed to protect his flock.

When Jesus needed an example of heedless humans, all he had to do was point to the sheep on surrounding hills. In John 10 he reminds his friends, and us, about the need for a sheepfold, a shelter built of rocks to keep away predators. He describes how the shepherd calls and numbers his flock as they enter a place of security for the night. He knows their names, and he knows ours. He assures them, and us, "I am the one true entrance into that safety."

But then in the same passage, Jesus changes the metaphor dramatically. "I am the Good Shepherd," he tells his hearers. He loves and cares for each one night and day. Like them, He is everything we need.

Oh, Jesus, Lord, Lamb of God, my Shepherd, how often I think I know what is best for me. How tempting it is for me to detour away from the pasture that you have provided for me, wanting autonomy, eager to find my own way. How patient you are, searching for me, rescuing me, bringing me home to you. I thank you with my whole heart. Amen.

Fifth Thursday of Lent

SCRIPTURE
Psalm 131, 132, 133, 140;
Jeremiah 26:1–16;
Romans 11:1–12;
John 10:19–42

WHEN I TRAVEL, I OFTEN CROSS INTERNA-tional borders. Driving to Canada from where I live just south of the border I need to have my passport and traveler's ID with me. There's enough suspicion and undercover crime going on that any country I enter needs to know who I am and that I have no criminal record and that I'm not importing drugs or weapons. Further, they have the option of searching my car for any forbidden goods. Once my true identity has been established, I'm allowed free access into my neighbor country.

Proof of identity is one of the common themes in today's lessons. When Jeremiah was required by God to warn the corrupt officials of dreadful coming judgment, at first he and his message were loudly rejected, even by the other priests and prophets. They were thoroughly appalled with him and his prophecy, which promised doom and destruction for them.

But Jeremiah was just as determined as they. His words had the ring of authenticity. He told them, "In truth, *the Lord sent me* to speak all these words in your ears." At this point the people themselves were convinced and decided to listen to him rather than the false prophets and priests.

God's authority was Jeremiah's passport.

Paul, in Romans 11, needed to establish his apostolic authority before he could testify to God's grace and forgiveness. Earlier in his life he'd experienced a radical shift in identity. To be counted as an apostle of Jesus, (which means "one sent with a message") he had to have been authorized by Jesus personally.

Remember, during his journey to Damascus in his role of a representative of the Jewish high priest, Paul had been commissioned to destroy all the Jesus followers he could find in that foreign city. Along the way he'd had the jolting experience of being thrown to the ground by a blinding light. That incident swung him around 180 degrees, turning him in a new direction, transformed from being a violent persecutor to an apostle who had been sent by Jesus. Even then he had to convince the Christian believers in Damascus that he had become one of them. He had to shed his old identity and start living and preaching out of the reality of the new one.

Even Jesus, in spite of all the miraculous events of healing that characterized his ministry, found himself the object of suspicion by the Jewish opposition of his day. As with many of our own present-day politicians, the easiest form of confrontation was to accuse their opponents of fraud and deceit: "You're lying." To that, Jesus simply responds, "Well, look at the evidence. Even if you don't believe me, look at what I've done. Pay attention to the man whose eyes are open. He's a new man! Pay attention to others I've healed; that should identify me as the Messiah. Then judge whether or not I have power from my Father."

> My heavenly Father, I admit my own blindness and skepticism. Because I long to take my identity from you as your representative, your ambassador, I pray for evidences of your power, divine surprises in my own life, that assure me you are with me and that I have been commissioned and redirected by you. In your Son Jesus's name, amen.

Fifth Friday of Lent

SCRIPTURE
Psalm 95, 22, 141, 143:1–12;
Jeremiah 32:27–34;
Romans 11:25–36;
John 11:28–44 or 12:1–10

NOW, HERE WE ARE, APPROACHING THE UNIQUE events of Holy Week. Can we in our day begin to move close to Jesus, his companions in the pain and dread that he, knowing what lay ahead of him, must have felt unbearably? Can we participate in it, begin to feel what he felt, begin to understand the dread he experienced, begin to travel along with him?

I believe we can. Identifying with what he must have felt will take meditative time—rereading the stories of the Passion, allowing them, through a sanctified imagination, to become vivid pictures in our own minds. In effect, we need to follow Jesus to Jerusalem, to Gethsemane. (It helps me that I've been there, among the ancient olives that are thought to have been alive when Jesus grieved and struggled there. It was raining, and I stood by those massive, stunted trunks and let the drops hanging from the leaves feel like tears.)

How deeply painful it is to be falsely accused. When that happens, everything in us cries out for justice, to be declared innocent, to be forgiven, to have the wrong erased.

I have a vivid memory from childhood. My parents thought I'd filched a coin from my younger brother's piggy bank. I denied it; I knew I hadn't done it. The parental belief that I'd added to my offense by lying, since lying was the Number One Sin in our household, made my wrongdoing seem even worse; the accusation itself felt like a verdict of guilt.

Even when I'd proved to my mother and father that I was telling the truth (my young sibling finally confessed he'd lost his little treasure himself), the sense of shame and false accusation clung to me for days. I felt tarnished.

Presumed guilt is heavy baggage.

From the foundation of the world Jesus had known the torment that lay ahead of him if he was to rescue humankind from the results of our failure. This task, of carrying the world's destiny, including all our misdeeds, on his shoulders all the way to an agonizing death, drove him ineluctably forward throughout his life. His friends couldn't bring themselves to believe that death could happen to him. He had to carry it all alone.

But Peter, who saw the drama unfold firsthand—the struggle, his own betrayal, the pivotal climax—could later write a letter about suffering. After all, he'd actually had a hand in the hurting by distancing himself from the accused. He'd learned a lot and he put it something like this, "Be happy when you suffer with Christ, knowing that it ends in glory."

Hurting? Living in anguish? No, thank you. That goes against our grain. We'd rather be comforted and rescued from pain. We shrink from the idea of hurt and shame.

Aha, but listen now to Paul, who had his share of suffering and tells us how closely it drew him to Christ. He tells us that he wants to "know Christ personally, experience his resurrection power, be a partner in his suffering."

> Lord Jesus, even two thousand years after you moved to heaven from our planet I want to be your companion, your disciple. You promise to be with me now, walking my life along with me. Put your strong arm around my shoulders. Teach me what your suffering means to me. And if need be, hold me close when I myself must suffer. Amen.

ON THE DAY BEFORE PALM SUNDAY, THE
Eastern Orthodox Church celebrates Lazarus Saturday,
commemorating the miraculous raising of Lazarus from the dead.
Although this is one of Jesus's most well-known miracles, many
Western Christians are not familiar with its connection to Holy
Week and Easter.

In the Gospel of John, where the Lazarus account is found,
Jesus's miracle of bringing Lazarus back to life and his later
return to Bethany to visit Lazarus and his sisters are the last
recorded events before the Lord's journey to Jerusalem on
Palm Sunday and his subsequent arrest and crucifixion. In
commemorating the miracle of Lazarus on the day before
Holy Week begins, the Orthodox calendar reminds us that
this "first Easter," as Lazarus's resurrection is sometimes
called, foreshadows the miracle to come, giving us a foretaste
of Easter joy that can carry us through Holy Week.

Lazarus Saturday marks the completion of the forty-day
fast known in the Orthodox Church as Great Lent. Holy
Week, the week following Palm Sunday and leading up to
Easter, is observed as a separate fast by Orthodox Christians,
and the feast days of Lazarus Saturday and Palm Sunday
serve as a joyful reprieve between the two fasts. Bright colors
are incorporated into the day's worship, and some dietary
restrictions are relaxed. In Greece, Lazarus Saturday is
celebrated with Lazarakia, a traditional spice bread shaped

into individual buns resembling men wrapped in burial cloths, their faces decorated with almonds or cloves. In some Eastern European countries, including Greece, Bulgaria, and Romania, children traditionally give a variety of musical and dramatic performances in their neighborhoods, singing songs about Lazarus from door to door, or performing dramatic reenactments of his resurrection. In return, members of the community give the children coins, eggs, cookies, or candy.

The connection between the Lazarus story and Jesus's own death and resurrection is evident in the Orthodox liturgy for this day, a resurrection liturgy normally reserved for Sundays. The gospel reading recounts the miracle of Jesus calling Lazarus out of the tomb, and hymns and prayers draw connections between Lazarus's resurrection and that of Christ, both of which bear the promise of a general resurrection. As one hymn from the service says, in the raising of Lazarus, God "confirm[s] the universal resurrection."

Christians in Jerusalem have observed the Saturday of Lazarus since ancient times by making a pilgrimage to Lazarus's hometown of Bethany. The tradition, likely begun by early pilgrims to the holy land from Constantinople, involved gathering together on the day before Palm Sunday and walking the roughly two miles from Jerusalem to Lazarus's hometown and tomb. There, the pilgrims would read the gospel account, not of the raising of Lazarus from the dead, but of Jesus's *return* to Bethany after report of the miracle had spread, just before his triumphal entry into Jerusalem. Reading about this second visit to Bethany, when Lazarus's restored life was remembered and celebrated, placed the memory of the miracle in proximity to the upcoming events of Palm Sunday and Holy Week. For these early Christians and for us, the celebration of Lazarus Saturday anticipates the Lord's coming victory over death.

SCRIPTURE

John 11:1–44;

Hebrews 13:1–8

A S KIDS IN SUNDAY SCHOOL WE LEARNED THAT the shortest verse in the Bible comes from this narrative in John's Gospel: "Jesus wept." That was it—a factoid to be learned for Bible quizzes.

Yet this remarkable story—the bringing back to life of Jesus's close friend Lazarus after a mortal illness—is one of the most detailed incidents in the New Testament, a full chapter of profound theological import. Perhaps in no other gospel story do we see God-human relationships brought into such full and powerful focus.

At one level this local drama also seems like a kind of movie trailer, a preview of Jesus's own death and final resurrection that was to happen very shortly in Jerusalem on a much larger stage,

In nearby Bethany Mary, Martha, and Lazarus, three siblings, were Jesus's intimate friends. It's clear that the Lord was at home in their home, a frequent guest. Hold that thought of loving relationship in mind. Then listen as John tells us how even Martha and Mary were puzzled and distraught at what happened in their time of crisis.

The writer of Hebrews confirms a principle of God's faithful friendship: "I'll never let you down, never walk off and leave you." The sisters had sent word that their brother was deathly sick, but Jesus hadn't come right away. Why did he wait? What was he thinking?

When he finally arrived and the sisters asked him about the delay, Jesus's response felt oddly unsatisfying. He seemed to be talking in universal rather than personal terms about living and dying and rising again. But what about their immediate crisis? Lazarus was four days dead. The sisters knew that Jesus was a miracle worker. Why had he waited?

Perhaps he is saying, "You're viewing your lives in terms of a few short days, frustrated by having to wait for answer. You have time rather than eternity in mind."

Or is a deep personal conundrum at work? It seems to me that both sides of Jesus's God-man nature are in collision here. As a man with "like passions as we are" he was "deeply moved," weeping with his friends, irate at what their brother's death had done to them.

Yet he had deliberately delayed coming so that they would all "see the glory of God." In this dramatic incident Jesus's humanity seems to clash painfully with his deity. His personal emotions conflict with his larger, life-giving purpose for the whole world. He had come to bring resurrection life that would encompass the whole world.

And then, of course, in the appointed time, he made it happen; "Lazarus, come forth!"

> Oh, Lord, I am so impetuous. I want immediate action and find it so hard to wait for you to do something. In my urgency to see things change for the better, I can't always see the big picture or view my relationships in terms of fulfilling your purposes.

Slow me down, push me deeper, enlarge my trust in your timing. May I never frustrate your purposes by imposing my own timetable. I pray this in your powerful name. Amen.

Beth Bevis
History of the Feast

Annunciation of the Lord

IN ADDITION TO THE EASTER AND CHRISTMAS cycles of the liturgical calendar, the church observes a cycle of individual feast days throughout the year, setting aside days to remember the saints, martyrs, and important events in Christian history. These days often overlap with other liturgical seasons, so that the celebration of a particular holy day can sometimes take place within the Lent-Easter or Advent-Christmas-Epiphany cycles. This is the case with the Annunciation of the Lord, which is observed on March 25 in both the East and West and often falls within Lent. When it does, this day marks an exception to the church's general ban on feasts during Lent.

The feast of the Annunciation of the Lord commemorates the first news of the Incarnation—the angel Gabriel's "annunciation" to the Virgin Mary that she will give birth to the Savior. The date for this feast was probably calculated by counting back nine months from the Nativity, which by the fourth century had been set at December 25. However, some church historians believe that March 25 may have already been designated as the date of the Lord's conception, and that the feast of the Nativity was then determined in relation to the Annunciation.

One reason early Christians might have chosen March 25 for the observance of Christ's conception is that it was also thought to be the date of the Crucifixion. Ancient Christian philosophy held that both the Incarnation and Passion would have happened on the same day as the creation of the world—which in ancient times was thought to be March 25, the date of the spring equinox, when daylight and darkness were perfectly equal (recalling the separation of day and night in Genesis). Thus, through God's mystical plan, all three events coincided in one symbolic day.

While the church now puts less emphasis on a literal concurrence of dates, the meaning of these three important elements of sacred history—Creation, Incarnation, and Atonement—can be brought to bear on our lives as they are collapsed in liturgical time. The proximity of the Annunciation to the spring equinox (which has shifted slightly to March 21), for example, means that this day is associated with new life: the return of birds in spring, the planting of new crops. Furthermore, the occurrence of this feast during Lent provides an opportunity to reflect on the meaning of both Incarnation and redemption, the two mysteries toward which the respective seasons of Advent and Lent are aimed. As we approach Easter, the celebration of Christ's conception reminds us that the great sacrifice of the cross and the glory of the Resurrection began with the Incarnation, when God chose to intervene in human history by becoming one of us.

The Annunciation is a Christological feast, rather than a Marian feast, meaning that the emphasis is on Jesus and his Incarnation. Nevertheless, the feast is intimately connected with Mary, the vessel of the Incarnation, and popular piety throughout history has tended to honor her on this day. At earlier times in church history, March 25 has been called the Annunciation of the Blessed Virgin Mary or the Annunciation of Our Lady; in England, it is still known as Lady Day. The

Swedish tradition of serving waffles on March 25 testifies to this history of "Our Lady's Day," now known as "Waffle Day" due to a confusion of the Swedish word for Our Lady, *Var Flu*, with the word for waffles, *Vaffla*. Another traditional Annunciation food is seed cake, a token of the new beginning represented not only by the feast's proximity to the spring equinox but also by the growth of Jesus in the womb. Thus the traditions of this day remind us of its position at the intersection of the two major cycles of the liturgical calendar—Christmas and Easter—introducing a sense of growing expectation and hope into the solemn season of Lent.

SCRIPTURE
Isaiah 7:10–14;
Psalm 40:5–11;
Hebrews 10:4–10;
Luke 1:26–38

O N THIS LENTEN DAY IN MARCH, NINE MONTHS before next Christmas, now, right after spring has sprung, we are called to celebrate the conception of Jesus, as if keeping company with Mary in her waiting time, living with her through the nine months before his birth. The commencement was preceded, of course, by the brilliant announcement voiced by a heavenly being. (I am so accustomed to connecting the Annunciation with Advent in December that this comes as a surprise. It feels a bit shocking. Really? Jesus wasn't conceived under a wreath of holly, with snow falling gently all around?)

But no. This was spring, always a time of lengthening light in Nazareth, and wherever we are. It was the season appointed for God to become enfleshed. And in his humanity Jesus, who was to be the world's Light, was like any other human baby. It took the seed of God nine long months in Mary's womb to grow into readiness to illuminate the world with his earth-shattering message of reversal and forgiveness. Think of it—a baby born with that kind of destiny, anticipating a life of almost universal rejection and a predetermined death sentence. But that life and death would slam the door on mortality and open up the golden possibility of eternal life for everyone.

So, this is meant to be a day of great rejoicing . . . but also of pondering. We may only guess how Mary, unmarried, felt at the news that she was to be a mother. Probably a young teenager, a thoughtful ponderer, but unversed in the ways of the world, she must have been astonished, with pangs of apprehension.

MARY CONSIDERS HER SITUATION
What next, she wonders,
with the angel disappearing, and her room
suddenly gone dark.

The loneliness of her news
possesses her. She ponders
how to tell her mother.

Still, the secret at her heart burns like
a sun rising. How to hold it in—
that which cannot be contained.

She nestles into herself, half-convinced
it was some kind of good dream,
she its visionary.

But then, part dazzled, part prescient—
she hugs her body, a pod with a seed
that will split her,
opening up a new w*orld*.

Most gracious God, you who opened your heavens to shine on our world, you who divinely surprised a young woman, you who sent through her your holy one, your anointed son, the dearest gift you could give, we listen again for your announcement to us. The virgin mother Mary, in whom your son was formed, gave you heartfelt praise for choosing her, of all the young women on earth, to carry Jesus in her body. We are also, by your Holy Spirit, enabled to bear Christ in us. In us, you are the hope of glory. How can we ever thank you enough? Now we, along with Mary, can sing a song that magnifies the Lord. Amen.

HOLY WEEK AND
EASTER

O N PALM SUNDAY, THE CHURCH REMEMBERS
Jesus's entry into Jerusalem just days before his death.
The gospels report that he arrived in the city on a donkey and
was greeted by an expectant crowd in a manner fit for a king:
the people waved palms in reverence and laid them in his path.
Acknowledging the one who had come to save, they shouted
"Hosanna," a word derived from the Hebrew scriptures, meaning
"Save, we pray."

From the earliest centuries of Christianity, the faithful have
remembered this day by incorporating palm branches into
worship. Fourth-century Christians in the holy land took part
in a palm procession, carrying palms from the Mount of Olives
into the city of Jerusalem, led by the bishop. The custom of a
palm procession probably originated even earlier in Alexandria,
Egypt, and Constantinople, and spread to Europe in the middle
ages. Today people throughout the Western world and in some
Eastern traditions have adapted this custom, using palms, olive
branches, or other local greenery that, in most traditions, has
been ceremonially blessed beforehand. Processionals begin
outside the church, or even at another church, where the priest
reads from the gospel account of Jesus's entry into Jerusalem.
Then the congregants and clergy process into the church
bearing palms. In most countries, a representation of Christ
is included as part of the procession, whether in the form of a
carved figure, a cross, the consecrated Eucharist, or the Bible.

The liturgical color for this day is red, the color of the Passion. On this last Sunday of Lent, we are closer than ever to the hope of Easter, but we are also entering into Holy Week, the most solemn week of the church year, set aside for remembering the events of Christ's last days. To acknowledge the beginning of Holy Week, some churches practice veiling on Palm Sunday (or during the vigil the night before), covering the altar and any images, statues, and crosses in dark fabric. A custom that stretches back to the middle ages, veiling imposes a sort of visual fast until the Easter vigil, when Christ is again revealed, his glory no longer hidden.

The Palm Sunday liturgy usually features an extended reading of the events of the Passion: Christ's last supper, betrayal, crucifixion, and death. Sometimes the congregation plays the part of the crowd, repeating everything from the initial "Hosanna" at Jesus's entry into Jerusalem to the condemning call to "crucify him!" Thus the celebratory feel of Palm Sunday is tempered by the knowledge that Jesus will soon be betrayed, and that those who now hail him as prophet and king will all have abandoned him by the time of his death.

After the Palm Sunday service, families take their palms home, often weaving them into the shape of a cross and displaying them year-round. In some churches, extra palms are saved until the next year, when they are burned for ashes to be used in the Ash Wednesday service. This practice emphasizes the interconnectedness of the church year—the sign of Christ's glory will become the physical reminder of our own humility and repentance, just as Christ's triumphal entry also hails his coming sacrifice.

Kathleen Norris

SCRIPTURE

Psalm 118:1–29;
Matthew 21:1–11;
Isaiah 45:21–25;
Psalm 22:1–21;
Philippians 2:5–11;
Matthew 26:35–27:54

THE HARD TRUTH ABOUT JOURNEYS IS THAT they demand that we embrace the unknown. We may embark with high hopes—accepting a marriage proposal, receiving news of a long-desired pregnancy—or with dread—the diagnosis is an inoperable and metastasized cancer—but we actually know very little about what will be demanded of us along the way, let alone what the outcome will be. Even the most humdrum day is a journey in this sense; upon rising in the morning we utter our prayers inattentively, as a demanding to-do list looms in our minds, but we can't foresee what we'll accomplish during the next twenty-four hours. We don't even know if this day, and those halfhearted prayers, will be our last. We count ourselves lucky if we can shove these dread thoughts aside and go about our business.

The difficult thing for us about Holy Week is that we think we do know all about the journey that Jesus and his disciples make from Palm Sunday to Easter. We believe we know how that journey ends; at least we've heard the story many times. Why do we have to hear it all again this year? Why go through yet another round of Holy Week liturgies?

To experience a meaningful Holy Week requires a great leap, not only of faith, but of imagination. We are asked to suspend our belief in the scientific method, which replicates experiments in order to replicate results. Our goal in Holy Week is different: we go through the familiar readings and rituals as we've done for years, but we're hoping that something new will emerge from those ancient stories. We are seeking something more than what's on the surface, and in order to find it we must begin by seeking something less, the humble but thorough joy of children.

On Palm Sunday we stand with the glad crowds who welcomed Jesus into Jerusalem shortly before the annual Passover rituals, marveling that our ordinary day has turned extraordinary, with a homegrown parade and singing, dancing in the streets, and the enthusiastic waving of palm branches. Even if we can barely recall the joyful faith of our childhood, we might recall the wonder of what the author of "Amazing Grace" calls "the hour I first believed."

We will need all the certainty of that faith, for our Palm Sunday readings quickly bring us to the heart of suffering. The Gospel takes us into Gethsemane, where Jesus is betrayed and arrested; soon we are hearing the story of his condemnation and death. Palm Sunday reminds us that our world can turn on a dime, that sudden changes in our circumstances can take us straight from praise to lament. But in exercising our God-given imagination, like the poet who first sang Psalm 22, we might also allow God to help us turn our most painful lament into praise.

This is the journey of Holy Week; this is the journey of our lives.

We praise you, Lord, for your gifts of childlike wonder and exuberant joy. We thank you for the hope you give us as we begin new ventures. Sustain us in that hope in the face of life's trials, and give us an enduring, joyful, and reverent faith in your promise of eternal salvation. May we always be willing to welcome you into our lives, finding in you both the king of glory and the faithful servant who suffers on our behalf. It is because of Jesus that we know we can look to you in our times of gladness and our times of grief. As we begin our Holy Week journey with Jesus and his disciples may we better understand your sacrificial love for us, and more willingly embrace all the sacrifices that your love calls us to bear. Hear us, Lord, as we pray in Jesus's name. Amen.

Monday of Holy Week

SCRIPTURE
Isaiah 42:1–9;
Psalm 36:5–10;
Hebrews 11:39–12:3;
Mark 14:1–9

TODAY'S READINGS ARE ALL ABOUT TRUST. Yesterday we heard the story of Jesus's death; today we are asked to trust that it was not in vain. We are asked to place our trust in a God whose purposes are greater than anything we can imagine, and in God's people, who constitute the "cloud of witnesses," those past and present people of faith, who bolster our own faith when we struggle to maintain it through the trials of life.

Drawing from the ancient self-revelation of God to Moses on Mt. Sinai, as the great "I am," we hear an echo of yesterday's "I am God, and there is no other." Isaiah and the psalmist insist that God's love is steadfast, that the God who created the universe is also committed to sustaining it and one day setting things right. Justice is God's goal; justice is what God intends to bring into the world. Our epistle and gospel readings remind us that God has chosen to include humanity in this great work, not only through the life, death, and resurrection of Jesus Christ, but through the lives of those who believe in him.

Isaiah's familiar prophecy of Jesus as "the suffering servant" gives us a model of how God works in our world, not through an arrogant assertion of power but through a patient hope. This prophecy is of great use to us in our Holy Week journey if we remember that it's not just about Jesus, but about us. Isaiah is describing any one of God's faithful who willingly and humbly takes on suffering as the cost of giving witness.

The concept of trust can be romanticized into irrelevance, but today's readings are dauntingly realistic. Seeking justice always comes at a cost. Jesus knows he must be put to death, but can endure the cross for the sake "of the joy to come." And that's a difficult proposition for us. We are willing to endure the pain of such things as childbirth and chemotherapy when we have evidence that the outcome is worth the struggle. But when there seems little reason to trust, when our lives are on the line and unwelcome changes obliterate our sense of God's presence, it is hard to rely on trust alone.

We do not journey through Holy Week alone; our "cloud of witnesses" includes Abraham and Sarah, Jacob, Ruth and Naomi, Mary and Joseph, all of whom were called by God to take uncertain and even dangerous paths in order to further God's purposes in bringing forth a savior. And surely the nameless woman of the Gospel is with us. In a Jerusalem tense with fear and political intrigue, she stands up for mercy. In a time of ugliness, surrounded by the brute force of empire, she stands up for beauty. Recognizing even before the disciples that Jesus will soon die, she commits a prophetic act of love, anointing him with fragrant oils, overcoming the stench of death with the scent of paradise.

We praise you, Lord, for the gift of trust. We thank you for the witness of so many people throughout the ages who have placed their trust in you and who now inspire us with their example of faithful and loving service. We thank you for your unfathomable love revealed to us in the scriptures, in the law, and in the life, death, and resurrection of your son Jesus Christ, in whose name we pray. Amen.

Tuesday of Holy Week

SCRIPTURE
Isaiah 49:1–6;
Psalm 71:1–12;
1 Corinthians 1:18–31;
John 12:27–38, 42–50

THE FIRST WORD WE HEAR TODAY IS "LISTEN," which at its root means to obey. If Monday's readings focused our attention on trust in God's steadfast love, today we consider more fully obedience as the proper response to all that God has given us.

Yesterday Isaiah described the suffering Messiah who at great cost accepts God's will for him. Today our understanding of that will expands as Isaiah reveals the great mission God intends for Jesus to fulfill. He is to be a light to all people, bringing salvation to all the earth. But the prophet reminds us that the word this savior brings is a sharp sword, cutting through our selfishness and desire for worldly status.

First Corinthians provides an especially vivid contrast between the world as we know it and as God intends it to be.

It's a prime example of divine humor: since humanity refused to know God through wisdom, God caught our attention with an act of such foolishness that we're still talking about it more than 2,000 years later.

But Paul is serious: he wants us to let go of what we think is important and consider what God values. Human strength cannot compare to the power of God's weakness in choosing death on the cross.

In the next passage Paul alters our course through Holy Week. If Jesus was called to such a "foolish" death we must now consider our own call. The ancient prophecies are new again, the passages of scripture that have become comfortably familiar now make us uneasy, demanding something of us that we may not want to give. We are the ones God is calling here and now, and all our advantages—whether by birth, acquired knowledge, or wealth—are nothing in God's sight. The only thing that matters is how we respond to God's call, and who we become in the process.

John's Gospel reveals a human Jesus who is tempted to ask God to spare him from certain death. But he knows that facing this hour, this trial and shameful death, is what God has called him to do. As at Jesus's baptism, a voice from heaven comes, this time to reveal that it is not Jesus who will be judged in the coming days, but our world.

Human foolishness and God's wisdom will meet on the cross.

We like things to make sense, and want to find meaning and purpose in our suffering. But we're puzzled by Jesus's assertion that only if he dies will he one day draw all people to himself. It confounds all reasoning. Our gospel is a sad commentary on our tendency to follow Jesus only so far. We would like to believe in him but value other things more: our good name, our place in the status quo, the "human glory" we can see rather than a divine glory that remains elusive. We continue our journey through Holy Week with heavy hearts, having been given much to ponder.

> We praise you, Lord, for the gift of wisdom that allows us to hear and obey your word. We thank you for the call you have given each of us, to spend our lives in your service. Help us to reject the folly that the world considers wisdom. Through the cross may we come to understand what you have called us to, and who you intend for us to be. In Jesus's name we pray. Amen.

Wednesday of Holy Week

SCRIPTURE
Isaiah 50:4–9a;
Psalm 69:7–15, 22–23;
Hebrews 9:11–15, 24–28;
John 13:21–35

ONCE AGAIN PROPHECIES ABOUT THE MESSIAH resound. Isaiah asserts that God has given him a tongue to teach, and to sustain the weary; an ear to listen for and obey God's word. Both the prophet and the psalmist remind us that even though accepting God's call brings abuse and contempt, this faithful servant cannot be shamed because it is God who upholds him. Again we see that divine wisdom and the world's folly are on a collision course.

We might readily accept this concept in the abstract, as a theological proposition, but Isaiah's Messiah addresses us directly, personally: "Who will contend with me? ... Who are my adversaries? ... Who will declare me guilty?" As we walk with Jesus and his disciples through Holy Week, these are the hard questions we need to ask ourselves. In what ways are we adversaries of Jesus? In what ways in our daily lives and in our churches do we fail to recognize him, or even betray him?

In Hebrews Jesus is named the mediator of a new covenant. We are asked to acknowledge our sinfulness, but also remember that Jesus has entered heaven not for his glory, but on our behalf. We also are given a prophecy: if the incarnation of Jesus and his death on the cross was meant to conquer sin, Jesus's second coming will bring eternal salvation to those who have waited for him, who have maintained their faith and hope that he will fulfill his promises to us.

But in the Gospel we are confronted anew with a familiar human frailty. The scene that John portrays is one of a betrayal that Jesus knows is coming, and indeed must come in order to bring about the death God has called him to. What illustrates so starkly the difference between God and us is how Jesus responds to this betrayal. He does not condemn Judas for his weakness or complain about the inability of his disciples to comprehend the necessity of his death.

Because he is the Son of God, as divine as he is human, Jesus responds to these betrayals with a total and unconditional love.

And he offers us a new commandment: to love one another as he has loved us.

We have only to look at ourselves and our Christian communities to see how well we are doing. Do we continue to betray this Jesus who incarnates love? Do we complain in hard times that God is not there for us and refuse to consider that in truth it is we who have refused to be present to God? Do we use our faith as a pretext for condemning others or status-seeking, or is it love that truly defines us as Christians? Does our modeling of God's love demonstrate to others that we are faithful followers of Jesus?

That is what Jesus has called us to, and what we must one day answer for. We are ready for Maundy Thursday.

> We praise you, Lord, for the many prophets you have inspired to proclaim your good news to the world. We thank you for the difficult questions they raise, as we consider how we so often betray Christ's message of peace and love. May we turn away from our human weakness as we seek to be true followers of Christ and heralds of your new covenant. We ask this in Jesus's name. Amen.

Beth Bevis
History of the Feast

Maundy Thursday

O N MAUNDY THURSDAY, THE CHURCH commemorates the Last Supper, the final meal that Jesus shared with his disciples before his betrayal. It was during this meal that, anticipating his death, Christ instituted the sacred ritual of remembrance that we now know as Holy Communion or the Eucharist. The synoptic gospels identify the Last Supper as the Jewish Passover meal, thus establishing a connection between Christ and the sacrificial Passover lamb. (John's Gospel suggests that the Passover feast coincided with Christ's death the next day, underscoring the sacrificial nature of his death.)

Christian theology has since interpreted Jesus's actions at the Last Supper in light of this connection to the festival of Passover; this is why he is sometimes referred to as the Paschal lamb or the Lamb of God. When he took the bread and wine of the paschal meal and identified them as his body and blood, Jesus instituted a new feast, a new covenant between God and his people. For this reason, one of the most important customs of the Maundy Thursday liturgy across denominational lines is the celebration of Communion.

"Maundy" is derived from the Latin word for commandment, "mandatum." It was on this day that Jesus gave his disciples what he called a "new command": "Love one another. As I have loved you, so you must love one another." Jesus's way of demonstrating this love at the Last Supper was to wash his disciples' feet, and today many churches offer Maundy Thursday foot-washing ceremonies. While the liturgy commemorates the institution of the sacrament of Communion, then, it also seeks to recreate the intimacy of Christ's last moments with his disciples, encouraging Christians to show others the self-sacrificing love that the Savior modeled in his last hours.

Readings for the liturgy are taken from the gospel accounts of this day's events—the Last Supper, the washing of the disciples' feet, Jesus's anguish in the garden of Gethsemane, and his betrayal, denial, and desertion by his disciples. In some churches, the end of the service features a stripping of the altar: cloth coverings and other nonpermanent ornamentations are removed, leaving the church bare in solemn anticipation of Good Friday. Parishioners then depart in silence. These rituals are a sign that we have entered what is known as the "Triduum," the last three days of Holy Week, during which preparation for Easter is intensified.

On this day in early church history, penitents who had received ashes at the beginning of Lent were invited back to the church to receive reconciliation. The green branches they carried may explain the traditional German name for this day: Green Thursday. Germans still eat green foods such as kale, spinach, and herbs on Green Thursday. The liturgical color for Maundy Thursday, however, is red—a color that signals the approach of the Passion. Greeks dye Easter eggs red on what they call "Red Thursday." In some liturgical churches, priests begin Maundy Thursday services wearing red robes, but in the middle of the service—at the celebration of the Eucharist—they change their vestments from red to white, signaling the church's joy over the institution of this sacrament. Thus, even at the beginning of the most solemn days of Lenten observance, we glimpse the gift Christ offered to his disciples by giving them a sacrament to remember him by, to make him present among them even after his death.

Kathleen Norris

Maundy Thursday

SCRIPTURE
Exodus 12:1–14a;
Psalm 78:14–20, 23–25;
1 Corinthians 11:23–26;
Luke 22:14–30

MAUNDY THURSDAY ENGAGES US IN DEEP remembrance. Looking at Moses and Aaron as they prepare the first Passover meal in Egypt, we better understand what acts of remembrance can mean for a people, and a religion. The Passover seder is still at the heart of Jewish faith and tradition. And in that Passover supper in Jerusalem depicted in Luke we witness the birth of our own Christian eucharistic meal.

But I want us to pay attention to what happened not in Egypt or Jerusalem, but in the desert of the Exodus, depicted in Psalm 78. God had worked many wonders for the people fleeing slavery in Egypt: parting the Red Sea, leading by fire and by cloud, drawing water from hard rock to quench their thirst. Still, as time goes by and the hardships continue, their faith in God's providence fails. In their hunger they doubt, and ask, "Can God spread a table in the wilderness?" In response, God sends them manna, bread from heaven.

We have been given so many great gifts in our lives, and in the lived traditions of our faith communities. The opportunity to gather in worship with others at the eucharistic table is a blessing beyond compare. But we often take it for granted, and when we face a desert journey—through illness, divorce, job loss, or any unwelcome change—we are still capable of asking if God can provide enough nourishment to see us through.

Even worse, we may be so distracted, enslaved by a desire for worldly goods, that we, like Jesus's disciples, fail to comprehend the gifts that are right before us. Any meal shared with those we love, whether it be at the altar or around a kitchen table, can be a foretaste of the heavenly feast to come, if only we will heed the words of the traditional Maundy Thursday hymn, "Ubi Caritas," which asks us to set aside our bitterness and quarreling and remember that "where charity and love are found, there is God."

Maundy Thursday is a time to remember what time spent with our loved ones truly means. Memory will give a glow to a meal shared with a friend or relative that turned out to be our last visit with them before they died. Our time with them is more precious now that they are gone. Jesus's disciples still don't seem to realize that this is their last night with him and that within a few hours he will be dying on a cross.

But on this night Jesus incarnates the patience and steadfast love of our God. Betrayed, and with his fate unacknowledged even by those closest to him, he does not respond with anger or threats of retribution. He offers the gift of himself, his body and blood, asking only that we remember him. God has prepared a table for us, once and forever. The eucharist is a past, present, and future reality, meant to nourish and sustain us.

Manna, indeed.

We praise you, Lord, for your gift of Christian community, and we thank you as we humbly and with reverence celebrate Christ's initiation of our communal eucharist. May we never fail to be grateful for the diverse people who make up the body of Christ, and sustain our faith in each other at times when we disagree. In the face of disappointments and betrayals keep us thankful for the new commandment Christ has given us, and help us to better love each other as he has loved us, with a sacrificial and unconditional love. As we struggle with doubts and fears, help us to trust that you will always provide the nourishment we need. We ask that you especially strengthen the faith of the many Christians around the world who are persecuted for daring to celebrate communion and the love of your son Jesus Christ, in whose name we pray. Amen.

Good Friday

O N GOOD FRIDAY, THE CHURCH COMMEMO-rates the death of Jesus, the event at the center of the Christian mystery of redemption. In most churches, the atmosphere is even more austere than on the other days of Lent. Lights are dimmed, decorations are spare, and music and bells are eliminated. Clergy enter services in silence. In the midst of this barrenness, the cross emerges as the central object of contemplation. In ancient times, Christians made Good Friday pilgrimages to Golgotha, where the bishop would unveil a relic of the true cross for all to behold.

Today's Good Friday services likewise encourage Christians to contemplate, revere, and even embrace the cross. Catholics attend a service called the Veneration of the Cross for that purpose. Another liturgy, known as the Three Hours service, focuses on the hours before Jesus's death; popular in many denominations, this service is held from noon until three o'clock, and features Jesus's seven utterances from the cross, such as his prayer for the forgiveness of his persecutors and his declaration, "It is finished."

On Fridays throughout Lent, especially Good Friday, many Christians attend the Stations of the Cross. This devotional practice features a series of fourteen images that guide churchgoers in prayerful contemplation of each scene of the Passion, from Jesus's arrest and condemnation to his burial. The tradition grew out of a practice of early pilgrims who visited the actual sites of the Passion; in the middle ages, artistic representations made it possible to recreate the experience in churches around the world.

Today the Stations of the Cross remains a popular Lenten service, especially among Anglicans and Catholics.

Good Friday is observed as a special fast, with some traditions calling for total abstinence from food until the afternoon. In Greece, Christians traditionally eat lettuce dipped in vinegar, recalling the sustenance offered to Jesus on the cross. Although food consumption on Good Friday is usually minimal, in England "hot cross buns" are a traditional Good Friday treat (they are also available throughout Lent in many places). Decorated with icing crosses, these pastries are possibly connected to a medieval practice of displaying the Eucharist, also stamped with a cross, for veneration on Good Friday.

In keeping with the fast, Catholics and Anglicans do not celebrate the Eucharist on this day, but in some cases do distribute elements consecrated on Maundy Thursday. Some Protestant churches, on the other hand, see Good Friday as a particularly suitable time to remember Christ's death through the practice of Communion.

The fasting, solemnity, and silence of Good Friday are complemented by traditions that make us eyewitnesses to the embodied, sensory spectacle of the cross. Passion plays, which originated in medieval times, are still performed for audiences around the world on Good Friday. These moving dramatizations center on the events of Jesus's last hours, especially his trial, crucifixion, and burial. Parades throughout Europe on Good Friday feature life-sized figures of Christ, his disciples, and the holy family, and evening funeral processions in Greece enact Christ's burial. As we approach Easter, it can be tempting to rush past Good Friday or to turn away from the cross in discomfort. But traditions like these help us to see the cross as the precursor to our joy, an inseparable part of the triumph that we celebrate at Easter.

Kathleen Norris

Good Friday

SCRIPTURE
Isaiah 52:13–53:12;
Psalm 22;
Hebrews 10:1–25;
John 18:1–40; 19:1–37

DEATH TESTS OUR FAITH, WHETHER WE ARE mourning the loss of a beloved family member or contemplating the suffering of Jesus on the cross. We can well imagine the disciples on Good Friday, stunned and disheartened by all that has happened to the dear friend they had dined with just the night before: arrest, a trial on trumped-up charges, and public execution.

What would they make of Jesus's lament from Psalm 22: "My God, my God, why have you forsaken me?" Would they be grateful that the book of Psalms allows us to express such an emotion before God, or would they find their trust in God shaken to the core?

Good Friday is a wake-up call, forcefully reminding us that suffering and death are real, and that even the son of God had to endure them. But Good Friday is also about our limited vision. When it comes to death, we are as shortsighted as Pilate, whose kingdom is built on power, the visible might of armies. He can't comprehend the kingdom Jesus represents, one grounded in truth and love. To us, death seems like an end, but for God it is the beginning of our return to the great love from which we came.

On Good Friday our faith in God's love is fortified by readings reminding us that Jesus's death continues the long story of salvation. Isaiah insists that God's servant, rejected by human society, is indeed the one who will astound the nations. In the letter to the Hebrews, citations from Psalm 40 and Jeremiah 31 help us understand Good Friday as part of the fulfillment of God's plan to write his law on our hearts. The Jesus who dies on the cross is also the king who will lead us to new life with God.

In the fourth century a Roman woman named Egeria made a pilgrimage to Jerusalem for Holy Week, and fortunately for us she kept a journal. Her account reveals that the faithful walked considerable distances each day, up and down the steep Jerusalem hills, to attend liturgies at sacred sites. Good Friday began with an all-night vigil at Gethsemane, followed by a long trek at dawn through the city to Golgotha. There the people assembled and listened to scripture readings for three hours.

Egeria writes, "First, whichever Psalms speak of the Passion are read. Next, there are readings from the apostles...whenever they speak of the Passion of the Lord. Next, the texts of the Passion from the Gospels are read. Then there are readings from the prophets, where they said that the Lord would suffer, and then they read from the Gospels, where He foretells his Passion."

The purpose of this, Egeria says, is that "the people are taught that nothing happened which was not prophesied, and that nothing was prophesied that was not completely fulfilled."

On Good Friday God created a kingdom, and we now live in that new reality.

We praise and thank you, Lord, for the gift of yourself on the cross. On this somber day of remembrance, as we contemplate Christ's suffering for us, help us find meaning in the wounds we endure and in the travails of the world you created. You have called us to accept our common mortality, and to serve one another in love; keep us firm in our faith as we are called to suffer for others. You have called us to keep telling the story of your salvation in the unjust and violent world we have made; help us see past the limits of our vision to your limitless love, which transcends death. In the prophecies, gospel stories, and apostolic witness of our scriptures may we always find consolation and hope, never faltering in our certainty that you are the God of a kingdom of justice and the author of life. Amen.

ALSO KNOWN AS GREAT SATURDAY IN EASTERN Europe or Saturday of Mourning in Germany, Holy Saturday is a time of mourning, stillness, and expectation. Today, on the eve of Easter, between death and resurrection, we confront the silence of the tomb. In observance of this silence, churches typically do not hold regular worship services during the day, reserving them until evening, when the Easter vigil begins. (For more on the Easter vigil, held on the evening of Holy Saturday, see the entry for Easter.)

While Holy Saturday is observed in solemnity, it is nevertheless a day of great anticipation as we draw closer to Easter and anticipate the end of the Lenten fast. It is customary for Easter preparations to begin on this day. In Eastern Europe, tables are decorated with flowers for the coming feast. In Greece, the lamb and Easter soup are prepared for the following day's meal. Greek families also bake a sweet bread called tsoureki on the morning of Holy Saturday, placing a red Easter egg at the center. All over Europe, families dye Easter eggs, and many people assemble a basket of Easter foods, bringing it to the church to have it blessed on Holy Saturday. The Easter baskets that are popular in America, filled with decorated eggs, sweets, and small gifts, reflect this European custom.

While regular services are often not held on Holy Saturday, some churches do offer devotional services, such as Stations of the Cross or Tenebrae, on the eve of Easter. Latin for "darkness,"

Tenebrae originated in the Middle Ages as an adaptation of the office of matins and lauds for Holy Thursday, Good Friday, and Holy Saturday, and has remained an important part of the observance of Holy Week not only in monasteries but also in various Protestant denominations. The traditional Tenebrae service begins with a set of fifteen lit candles, which are placed on a triangular candlestick known as a "hearse." Scriptures are read or chanted, with responses from the congregation, while one by one the candles are extinguished. When only one is left burning, representing Christ, it is taken behind the altar, where it remains hidden until the end of the service. The progressive snuffing of candles, in addition to creating a sense of growing darkness, represents the gradual desertion of Jesus by his disciples. While the one candle remains hidden, we are reminded of Christ's death and burial—his hiddenness. Brought back into sight at the end of the Tenebrae, the candle signifies our hope in the coming resurrection.

The service is dominated by the interplay of darkness and light, but sound plays an important role as well. A loud noise signals the end of the service: when the Tenebrae draws to a close, clergy and congregants create a clamor by beating their hands on hard surfaces or stomping their feet. This tradition probably originated because the sound made by the closing of chant books seemed especially loud during the Triduum, when bells and other music were disallowed; eventually the noise gained allegorical significance as a reminder of the turmoil at Christ's death: thunder, earthquakes, and the tearing of the temple veil. Having glimpsed the hope of the Resurrection represented by the return of the final candle, parishioners depart the Tenebrae service in silence, dismissed, for now, with the commotion of Christ's death into the silence of the grave.

Kathleen Norris

Holy Saturday

SCRIPTURE
Job 14:1–14;
Psalm 31:1–5;
1 Peter 4:1–8;
Matthew 27:57–66

A S A BREAD BAKER I HAVE COME TO SAVOR THE still time when the yeast, flour, and water are becoming dough. The first time my young nieces helped me make bread, they seemed surprised that we were going to let the dough sit for a time. After an hour they were amazed at how large the dough had become in its bowl, and a little frightened to see their arms disappear into it as we began to punch it down. They were clearly dubious about this mess turning into loaves of bread.

Holy Saturday is a day for expectant silence, a day to disconnect from the noise of the Internet, cell phones, television. We might reflect, with Job on the meaning of mortality, and with the psalmist surrender ourselves to God's protection. Psalm 31 is commonly used at funerals and graveside committals, and in the stillness of Holy Saturday we can find the awful quiet that comes after such a service, and feel the emptiness within.

Joseph of Arimathea demonstrates great kindness, offering to place Jesus's body in a tomb he had intended for himself. Pilate orders the body to be given to Joseph and, at the request of frightened religious authorities, commands that the tomb be made secure. From his point of view, this is all it takes to make it so. The tomb is sealed, soldiers will guard it: end of story.

But for those who recognize that they are accountable to a power greater than that of any human authority, the story is just beginning. When we are grieving, new life seems impossible. But hints of resurrection abound, in the stirrings of spring, when seemingly dead branches come to life and fill with songbirds returned from winter migrations. As Job observes, even when a tree is cut down, its shoots can sprout again.

Holy Saturday reflects the in-between time in which we live, between life and death. If Job asks the central question that haunts all humanity: "If mortals die, will they live again?" in the letter to Peter we are admonished to live now as if our eternal life were certain. This is the realism of Christian faith, to know that the end is coming, as no one escapes death. We can choose to live in fear and allow selfish concerns to dominate us, or live thankfully, offering hospitality, kindness, and love to others, with whom we share a common mortality.

I knew what to expect from that bread dough, but my nieces did not. To them it was utter mystery. Karl Rahner, writing on Holy Saturday in *The Great Church Year*, states that "the virtue of our daily life is the hope which does what is possible and expects God to do the impossible. To express it somewhat paradoxically...the worst has already happened; we exist, and even death cannot deprive us of this. Now is the Holy Saturday of our ordinary life, but there will also be Easter, our true and eternal life."

We praise and thank you, Lord, for the uncertain, in-between times in our lives when we can be still and know that you are God. We praise and thank you for the hidden wonders of each day. We praise and thank you for acts of kindness, great and small, that serve to bring about your kingdom. We praise and thank you for the courage to place ourselves under your protection, not allowing fear to have the upper hand. We praise and thank you for your patience with our weakness, for being willing to work in and through us in ways we do not understand. We praise and thank you for our emptiness, which will one day be filled with your love. We praise and thank you for the silent wonders you work in us, preparing us for a life that will find its completion in you. Amen.

ASTER, THE CELEBRATION OF JESUS'S RESURREC-
tion from the dead, is the oldest and most important feast
of the church year. From as early as the second century, the celebration of Easter has coincided with the Jewish festival of Passover. According to the gospels, the Resurrection took place on the
Sunday after the Passover feast, and this connection between the
two feasts has shaped the church's understanding of Easter as itself a kind of Passover—a divine act of forgiveness and liberation.
The traditional name for Easter is Pascha, Greek for Passover.
Having traveled through a season of repentance and fasting, we
celebrate today the forgiveness and new life achieved for us by
Christ's "Passover"—his death and resurrection.

Families around the world break the Lenten fast with
elaborately prepared feasts. Eggs, at one time forbidden during
Lent (and still prohibited in Orthodox Lent), are a special
Easter treat in both East and West. Likewise, each aspect of the
Easter liturgy offers a "feast" for the senses: images that have
been covered during Holy Week are unveiled, Lenten purple
is exchanged for bright white, incense fills the sanctuary, and
parishioners once again proclaim the "Gloria" and "Alleluia."
Some congregations incorporate a traditional Easter greeting
in which the minister calls out, "Christ is risen," to which
congregants respond, "He is risen, indeed!" Services feature
joyful music, including the return of bells and the organ where
they have been silenced.

The symbolism of Easter liturgy centers on light. It was at dawn that Christ's followers discovered the empty tomb, and Christian tradition thereafter associated the direction of the east with the Resurrection and Second Coming. Sunrise services, popular in churches of various denominations, draw on this symbolism by taking place outside just before dawn.

Likewise, the Easter vigil—the oldest known Easter liturgy still celebrated today—emphasizes the coming of light. The vigil is a night service held on the eve of Easter. It begins in darkness with the lighting of an Easter fire and a paschal candle. A minister, carrying the candle into the church, proclaims "Lumen Christi," the light of Christ. Congregants then light their own candles from the Easter candle until the sanctuary is brightened. The Easter vigil features Old Testament readings, including the creation, the story of Abraham and Isaac, and the exodus. These readings culminate with the cross and Resurrection, thus locating Easter in the context of God's saving action toward humanity throughout biblical history.

Since its origin in ancient Jerusalem, the climax of the Easter vigil has been the baptism of adults who have been preparing throughout Lent to be received into the church. Catechumens may be confirmed at this time, as well, and all members of the church participate in a communal renewal of their baptismal vows, followed by a sprinkling of water. While these rites of Christian initiation are especially important aspects of Easter worship in Catholic, Anglican, Orthodox, and Lutheran churches that celebrate the Easter vigil, various Protestant denominations also perform baptisms at Easter, seeing it as a meaningful time to express the new life of the convert, who, in

Saint Paul's words, is buried with Christ in baptism and raised with him to new life (Romans 6:4).

In liturgical churches, the Easter candle remains lit throughout the season of Easter until Pentecost, when the church commemorates the descent of the Holy Spirit as described in the book of Acts. Because the day of Pentecost marks the birth of the Christian church and the end of the Easter season, we extinguish the paschal candle and enter into a new season characterized by the guidance of the Holy Spirit, the work of the church in the world, and the rhythms of everyday life: the season of Ordinary Time.

Kathleen Norris

Easter / Pascha

SCRIPTURE
Exodus 14:10–14, 21–25; 15:20–21;
Psalm 118:14–17, 22, 24;
Acts 10:34–43;
John 20:1–18

O UR FIRST READING TRANSPORTS US TO A
frantic scene. The Israelites have fled Egypt with Pharaoh
and his army in pursuit. Masking their fear with sarcasm, they ask
Moses, "Was it because there were no graves in Egypt that you
have taken us away to die in the wilderness?" If they were slaves
in Egypt, at least they were secure, not faced with a dangerous
desert journey.

I find it appropriate to begin the Easter readings with this
vivid depiction of doubt, because I suspect that the Israelite's
bitter question is one most of us have asked in the deserts of our
own lives, when powerful enemies or painful events threaten
to overwhelm us, and the devil we know, even if it enslaves us,
seems preferable to the freedom offered by God. At such times
even powerful reassurance—"The Lord will fight for you, and
you have only to keep still"—can seem absurd.

God provides the Israelites with a path through the sea so
that they cross safely. The lesson we are meant to take from
this, and that today's other readings reinforce, is that God never
brings us to a desert in order to let us die. God intends for his
beloved to thrive and for the psalmist to assert, "I shall not die,
but I shall live, and recount the deeds of the Lord."

The retelling of the salvation story is essential in keeping our faith alive. Paul's epistle reminds us that we are called to be witnesses of these great events and to pass them on.

I find echoes of the Exodus story in Mary Magdalene's frantic response to discovering that the body of Jesus is no longer in the tomb. She runs off to alert the disciples. During times of uncertainty, we often want to get busy, doing something rather than nothing. It is only when Mary returns to the tomb, standing still and weeping helplessly, that she encounters Jesus. At first, preoccupied with grief, she does not recognize him. Only when he speaks to her does she realize it is the teacher himself, somehow risen from the dead. Mary returns to the disciples to announce that she has seen the Lord, thus earning the title bestowed on her by the ancient church, "apostle to the apostles."

Mary's telling of the good news is a task she has passed on to us. How do we recognize that we have seen the Lord, and how do we reveal this glorious truth to others? How do we dare speak of salvation and hope in a world so full of injustice, hatred, violence, and deadly accident?

This is the challenge and the mystery of Easter. For me it helps to remember that the victory song of Miriam is one of the most ancient in our scriptures. For many thousands of years the faithful have been able to stand tall and sing: "Sing to the Lord, for he has triumphed gloriously."

We thank and praise you, Lord, for the gift of your victory over death, for the gift of holy awe that comes upon us as we enter into our Easter joy. Christ has passed from death to life; may we always know you as our way through the desert, our food and drink as we thirst. You are our safe passage through treacherous waters and the home that awaits us at the end of all our journeys. In our doubts and in the pressures of our busy lives, we seem to lose you. Help us remember that you are always with us and that your way is always before us; we have only to pay attention to hear you call us by name. Teach us to recognize you in one another and with deep gratitude continue to bear witness to the life and hope with which you sustain the world. Amen.

Notes

Shrove Tuesday

16 *Joy then is … under the sun*   Ecclesiastes 8:15 (author's rendering)

16 *There is a season … time for dancing*   Ecclesiastes 3:1, 4 (NJB)

17 *The time has come … the good news*   Mark 1:15 (author's rendering)

17 *life and life more abundantly*   John 10:10 (author's rendering)

17 *new heaven and a new earth*   Revelation 21:1 (NASB)

Ash Wednesday

20 *Remember that you are dust*   see Genesis 3:19

22 *to rend our hearts and not our garments*   Joel 2:13 (NASB)

22 *Where is their God?*   Joel 2:17b (NASB)

22 *God, as it were, is appealing to the world through us*   2 Corinthians 5:20 (author's rendering)

22 *Now is the acceptable time! Now is the day of salvation!*   2 Corinthians 6:2 (NASB)

22 *By changing sides … us have lived*   2 Corinthians 5:21 (author's rendering)

22 *we might become the very holiness of God*   2 Corinthians 5:21 (author's rendering)

Thursday after Ash Wednesday

25 *You cannot serve both God and mammon*   Luke 16:13 (KJV)

26 *Whoever wishes to save his life must lose it, and whoever loses his life … will save it*   Luke 9:24 (NASB)

26 *The fact that life and death are 'not two' is extremely
difficult to grasp, not because it is so complex, but because
it is so simple* Ken Wilber, *The Spectrum of Consciousness*
(Wheaton, IL Quest, 1993), 110.

Friday after Ash Wednesday

27 *This is the fasting ... on your own* Isaiah 58:6, 7 (author's
rendering)

Saturday after Ash Wednesday

30 *You will be ... for your sake* Isaiah 58:11, 12 (author's
rendering)

32 *sons of thunder* Mark 3:17

32 *The healthy do not need a doctor, sick people do* Matthew
9:12 (author's rendering)

First Week of Lent

36 *you will surely die* Genesis 2:17 (NASB)

39 *Beware of saying ... power for me* Deuteronomy 8:17, 18
(author's rendering)

39 *The one who ... brothers [and sisters]* Hebrews 2:11 (author's
rendering)

41 *I stayed forty days and forty nights on the mountain, with
nothing to eat or drink* Deuteronomy 9:9 (NJB)

41 *It is not for any goodness of yours that I am doing this*
Deuteronomy 9:6 (author's rendering)

42 *a confidence that we can glory in* Hebrews 3:6 (author's
rendering)

42 *temple of his body* John 2:21 (NASB)

42 *"temples" of God and the Holy Spirit* 1 Corinthians 3:16–17,
6:19; 2 Corinthians 6:16; Ephesians 2:21–22

43 *turning my Father's house into a marketplace* John 2:16
(author's rendering)

44 *blot out their name from under heaven*   Deuteronomy 9:14
(NASB)

45 *Everyday, as long ... encouraging one another*   Hebrews 3:13
(author's rendering)

45 *Keep a grasp ... the very end*   Hebrews 3:14 (author's
rendering)

46 *the mind of Christ*   1 Corinthians 2:16 (NASB)

47 *Take no notice ... and their sin*   Deuteronomy 9:27 (NJB)

48 *God sent not ... might be saved*   John 3:17 (KJV)

49 *On these grounds ... into the light*   John 3:19-21 (author's
rendering)

49 *Christ likes us ... into his arms*   Simone Weil, *Waiting for God*
(New York: HarperCollins, 1951), 27.

50 *circumcision of the heart*   Deuteronomy 10:16 (NASB)

50 *God has made you as numerous as the stars of heaven*
Deuteronomy 10:22 (NASB)

51 *only lay claim ... given from above*   John 3:27 (author's
rendering)

52 *he must grow greater ... must grow smaller*   John 3:30
(author's rendering)

52 *the Father loves the Son and has entrusted everything to his
hands*   John 3:35 (NJB)

54 *He can sympathize ... limitations of weakness*   Hebrews 5:2
(author's rendering)

54 *two short places in Hebrew scriptures*   Genesis 14:17–20;
Psalm 110:4

55 *I am he*   John 4:26 (NASB)

55 *If you but knew the gift of God*   John 4:10 (NASB)

Second Week of Lent

64 *I am thirty-five ... mortal drinks [from]*   Jane Smiley, *The Age
of Grief* (New York: Anchor Books, 1987), 132.

67 *Living Water ... Amen*   In Elizabeth Roberts and Elias
Amidon, eds., *Life Prayers from Around the World* (San
Francisco: HarperSanFrancisco, 1996), 279.

68 *I remember the … through the wilderness*   Jeremiah 2:2 (NIV)

68 *God will assert … be faithful throughout*   Jeremiah 31:3–45
    (author's rendering)

69 *God is described … of treating women*   Renita Weems,
    *Battered Love: Marriage, Sex, and Violence in the Hebrew
    Prophets* (Minneapolis: Fortress Press, 1995), 72–73, 93–113,
    passim.

70 *God, we confess that … the world. Amen*   The Community
    of Our Lady for Perpetual Help, Salem, Virginia. "Prayer to
    end domestic violence." Accessed June 30, 2013. http://www.
    olphsalem.org/ministries/justice_peace/domvioawa/text23.html.

71 *at whatever point … the same things*   Romans 2:1 (author's
    rendering)

72 *First remove the … the first stone*   Matthew 7:5, John 8:7
    (author's rendering)

73 *Therefore the earth … above grow dark*   Jeremiah 4:28 (NIV)

74 *The heavens declare … of the world*   Psalm 19 (NIV)

74 *Earth is suffering … in the meantime*   Laurie J. Braaten,
    "Earth Community in Joel: A Call to Identify with the Rest
    of Creation," in Norman C. Habel, and Peter Trudinger,
    Exploring Ecological Hermeneutics (Atlanta: Society of Biblical
    Literature, 2008), 69–73.

77 *Who goeth in … strengthen my decays*   George Herbert,
    "Lent," in *George Herbert: the Complete English Poems*,
    edited by John Tobin, 79 (London: Penguin Books, 2004).

77 *The result and … life, into humus*   USA Gardener,
    "Gardening & Horticultural Glossary." Accessed June 30,
    2013. *usagardener.com/glossary-files/glossary-c.php*.

79 *The building of … is our protection*   Rabbi Samson Raphael
    Hirsch,   http://www.ou.org/torah/article/rabbi_weinrebs_
    torah_column_sukkot#.UcylSGeQjxU.

Third Week of Lent

86 *For many, if ... of their meaning* Father Alexander
Schmemann, *Great Lent* (Crestwood, NY: Saint Vladimir's
Seminary Press, 1996), 31–33.

88 *like our father ... as righteousness* Romans 4:1–12 (*The
Eastern/Greek Orthodox New Testament* [based on The
Patriarchal Text] New Rome Press, 2012)

89 *Whoever speaks from ... unrighteousness in him* John 7:14
(*The Eastern/Greek Orthodox New Testament* [based on The
Patriarchal Text], New Rome Press, 2012)

91 *Enter eagerly into ... which to ascend* Saint Isaak of Syria
(Boston: Holy Transfiguration Monastery, 2011), 121.

92 *O Lord and ... of ages. Amen* Saint Ephrem of Syria
(traditional adaptation of the Orthodox Church, see Father
Alexander Schmemann, *Great Lent* [Crestwood, NY: Saint
Vladimir's Seminary Press, 1996]), 34.

93 *Suffering produces perseverance; perseverance, character;
and character, hope* Romans 5:3, 4 (*The Eastern/Greek
Orthodox New Testament* [based on The Patriarchal Text],
New Rome Press, 2012)

94 *Now I rejoice . . . which is the Church* Colossians 1:24
(*The Eastern/Greek Orthodox New Testament* [based on The
Patriarchal Text], New Rome Press, 2012)

94 *What is a ... in his heart* Saint Isaak of Syria, *The
Ascetical Homilies of Saint Isaac the Syrian* (Boston: Holy
Transfiguration Monastery, 1984), 344–45.

96 *As sin entered . . . all sinned* Romans 5:12 (*The Eastern/
Greek Orthodox New Testament* [based on The Patriarchal
Text], New Rome Press, 2012)

97 *Repentance is the ... dawns within us* Saint Isaak of Syria

100 *It is not ... a liturgical being* Paul Evodkimov, *The Sacrament
of Love* (Crestwood, NY: Saint Vladimir's Seminary Press,
1985), 61–62.

108 *the mother of us all* Galatians 4:26 (KJV)

Fourth Week of Lent

Fifth Week of Lent

148 *Be happy when you suffer with Christ, knowing that it ends in glory* Philippians 3:8–11 (author's rendering)

148 *know Christ personally, experience his resurrection power, be a partner in his suffering* Philippians 3:10 (THE MESSAGE)

151 *Jesus wept* John 11:35 (RSV)

151 *I'll never let you down, never walk off and leave you* Hebrews 13:5 (The Message)

152 *like passions as we are* James 5:17 (KJV)

152 *Lazarus, come forth* John 11:43 (KJV)

Holy Week

170 *self-revelation of God ... "I am"* Exodus 3:14

170 *I am God, and there is no other* Isaiah 46:9 (NRSV)

175 *Who will contend ... declare me guilty?* Isaiah 50:8 (NRSV)

177 *Love one another ... love one another* John 13:34 (NIV)

183 *It is finished* John 19:30 (KJV)

185 *My God, my God, why have you forsaken me?* Psalm 22:1 (NRSV)

186 *First, whichever Psalms ... not completely fulfilled* Egeria, *Egeria: Diary of a Pilgrimage* (New York: Newman Press, 1970), 112.

192 *If mortals die, will they live again?* Job 14:14 (NRSV)

192 *the virtue of ... and eternal life* Karl Rahner, *The Great Church Year* (New York: Crossroad Publishing Company, 1994), 169.

199 *Was it because ... in the wilderness?* Exodus 14:11 (NRSV)

199 *the Lord will ... to keep still* Exodus 14:14 (NRSV)

199 *I shall not ... deeds of the Lord* Psalm 118:17 (NRSV)

200 *Sing to the ... has triumphed gloriously* Exodus 15:21 (NRSV)

Acknowledgments

There are too many people who should be listed here: family, friends, patrons, mentors, and colleagues, all of whom have walked with me down this path of discovery into the meaning of Lent and Easter. Each of these individuals understands and embodies love, loyalty, wisdom, and presence. They have journeyed with me through the death of dreams and danced with me in the celebration of fulfilled aspirations.

In the Lenten seasons of these past few years a few close friends have (often unknowingly) encouraged, inspired, prodded, and enabled me. These include Dean and Shirley, David and Marnie, Jack and Shirley, Scott and Mary, Mark and Karen, Volker and Elke, Sandy, Norm, Charlie, Rod, David J., Baxter, Paul, and David G.

In particular, I am grateful to Gregory Wolfe, who has continued to be a patient and gifted companion in the creation of this book. To risk a cliché: this book would not exist without him and the community of artists and writers he has built through *Image* journal. In the midst of his extraordinary literary activities, it is a great kindness that he has chosen to be so critically involved in the creation of *God For Us*. So I am delighted that *Image* has agreed to be a sponsor of this volume.

I would like to thank the contributors to this volume, whose influence on the spiritual formation of so many has been so profound. I am also grateful to Sara Arrigoni for her labors in copyediting the manuscript.

Heartfelt thanks to David Goa and Vladika Lazar (and the late Alexander Schmemann) for gently leading me to the ecclesial home that has had such a great influence in my life.

I am most grateful to David J., Brian and Ellen, and Herb and Erna, Laurie and Lilly, Geraldine, Leslie, Tom and Karen, Jack and Shirley, Peter, and Ken and Ruth, who made the publication of this book possible. Their generosity—in the midst of their ongoing commitment to various worthy endeavors—speaks to the depth and breadth of their desire for renewal in the church and in the world.

And, finally, to Andrea, my wife of eighteen months, who has so patiently and fully embraced a complicated husband who stumbles down the path of learning to hold things lightly. She remains my constant inspiration, comfort, and source of human (and often divine) kindness. —GREG PENNOYER

Contributors

BETH BEVIS teaches writing at Indiana University, where she is a PhD candidate in English. Her writing has appeared in *Image* and the *Indiana Review*.

SCOTT CAIRNS is a professor of English at the University of Missouri and director of Writing Workshops in Greece. His poems and essays have appeared in *Poetry*, *Image*, *Paris Review*, *The Atlantic Monthly*, *The New Republic*, etc., and both have been anthologized in multiple editions of *Best American Spiritual Writing*. He received a Guggenheim Fellowship in 2006, and is completing work on a new poetry collection, *Idiot Psalms*, and a translation of selections from *The Philokalia*, which will be *Descent to the Heart*.

KATHLEEN NORRIS is the author of *Acedia & Me*, *The Cloister Walk*, *Amazing Grace: A Vocabulary of Faith*, *Dakota: A Spiritual Geography*, and *Journey: New & Selected Poems*. She is an editorial advisor to the *Christian Century* and *Give Us This Day*.

RICHARD ROHR is a Franciscan priest of the New Mexico Province. He founded the Center for Action and Contemplation in Albuquerque in 1987, where he now serves as dean of their Living School. He is a well-known author and spiritual director, and traveled internationally as an ecumenical teacher for over forty years.

RONALD ROLHEISER is a Roman Catholic priest, a member of the religious community The Missionary Oblates of Mary Immaculate (OMI). In 2005, Rolheiser began his current ministry as the President of the Oblate School of Theology in San Antonio, Texas. Fr. Rolheiser frequently lectures on contemporary spirituality, religion and culture, and mysticism and is an award-winning author. His weekly column "In Exile" is carried in more than 100 newspapers worldwide.

JAMES CALVIN SCHAAP taught literature and writing at Dordt College for thirty-seven years before retiring recently. He has published many short stories and several novels, including *Romey's Place*, *In the Silence There Are Ghosts*, *The Secrets of Barneveld Calvary*, and *Touches the Sky*, as well as two books of meditations, *Sixty at Sixty* and *Honest to God*. He and his wife, Barbara, live in the country just outside of Alton, Iowa.

LUCI SHAW is a poet, essayist, lecturer, and writer-in-residence at Regent College in Vancouver, B.C. She has authored over thirty books. Widely anthologized, her writing has appeared in *Image, Weavings, Books & Culture, The Christian Century, The Southern Review,* and others. She is a 2013 recipient of the Denise Levertov Award.

LAUREN F. WINNER is an Episcopal priest and author of *Girl Meets God* and *Still: Notes on a Mid-faith Crisis*. She lives in North Carolina.

Editors

GREG PENNOYER works with a Canadian think tank, Cardus, where he directs the Faith in Canada 150 program. He has been a consultant on strategic planning, fundraising, and project development. He is the co-founder of the Centre for Cultural Renewal (Ottawa, Canada) and was the project director for a new online exhibition "Uencounter.org" that seeks to explore what it means to be human through 24 images on the life and teachings of Christ.

GREGORY WOLFE is editor of *Image*, one of America's leading quarterly journals. He serves as Writer in Residence and Director of the low-residency MFA in Creative Writing program at Seattle Pacific University. His literary imprint, Slant Books, is published by Wipf & Stock. Wolfe's books include *Beauty Will Save the World*, *Intruding upon the Timeless*, and *The Operation of Grace*. He has served as a judge for the National Book Awards.

ABOUT PARACLETE PRESS

WHO WE ARE

Paraclete Press is a publisher of books, recordings, and DVDs on Christian spirituality. Our publishing represents a full expression of Christian belief and practice—from Catholic to Evangelical, from Protestant to Orthodox.

We are the publishing arm of the Community of Jesus, an ecumenical monastic community in the Benedictine tradition. As such, we are uniquely positioned in the marketplace without connection to a large corporation and with informal relationships to many branches and denominations of faith.

WHAT WE ARE DOING

PARACLETE PRESS BOOKS | Paraclete publishes books that show the richness and depth of what it means to be Christian. Although Benedictine spirituality is at the heart of all that we do, we publish books that reflect the Christian experience across many cultures, time periods, and houses of worship. We publish books that nourish the vibrant life of the church and its people.

We have several different series, including the best-selling Paraclete Essentials and Paraclete Giants series of classic texts in contemporary English; Voices from the Monastery—men and women monastics writing about living a spiritual life today; award-winning poetry; best-selling gift books for children on the occasions of baptism and first communion; and the Active Prayer Series that brings creativity and liveliness to any life of prayer.

MOUNT TABOR BOOKS | Paraclete's newest series, Mount Tabor Books, focuses on liturgical worship, art and art history, ecumenism, and the first millennium church, and was created in conjunction with the Mount Tabor Ecumenical Centre for Art and Spirituality in Barga, Italy.

PARACLETE RECORDINGS | From Gregorian chant to contemporary American choral works, our recordings celebrate the best of sacred choral music composed through the centuries that create a space for heaven and earth to intersect. Paraclete Recordings is the record label representing the internationally acclaimed choir Gloriæ Dei Cantores, praised for their "rapt and fathomless spiritual intensity" by *American Record Guide*; the Gloriæ Dei Cantores Schola, specializing in the study and performance of Gregorian chant; and the other instrumental artists of the Gloriæ Dei Artes Foundation.

Paraclete Press is also privileged to be the exclusive North American distributor of the recordings of the Monastic Choir of St. Peter's Abbey in Solesmes, France, long considered to be a leading authority on Gregorian chant.

PARACLETE VIDEO | Our DVDs offer spiritual help, healing, and biblical guidance for a broad range of life issues including grief and loss, marriage, forgiveness, facing death, bullying, addictions, Alzheimer's, and spiritual formation.

Learn more about us at our website:
www.paracletepress.com or phone us
toll-free at 1.800.451.5006

SCAN
TO
READ
MORE

You may also be interested in . . .

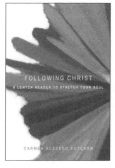

Following Christ
A Lenten Reader to Stretch Your Soul

Carmen Acevedo Butcher
ISBN 978-1-55725-540-2 $16.99, Paperback

In this unique daily reader for the season of Lent, short readings from extraordinary Christians will open windows on your spiritual life, allowing fresh air to burst in.

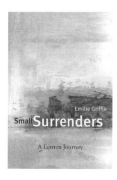

Small Surrenders
A Lenten Journey

Emilie Griffin
ISBN 978-1-55725-642-3 $16.99, French-flap paperback

Using ancient and modern texts as inspiration for these daily devotions for Lent, Emilie Griffin nurtures and guides us into a deeper knowledge of ourselves and God. We discover that Lent is an opportunity to joyfully put ourselves in God's hands.

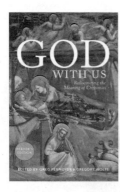